David Campbell

Stone in Traditional Architecture

Schiffer Publishing Ltd

4880 Lower Valley Road   Atglen, Pennsylvania 19310

Acknowledgments

My thanks to:

JUAN OCAMPO ROSALES, stonecutter in Taxco, Mexico, who welcomed me as a guest at his home in 1977, and taught me the bases of stonecutting and sculpture;

STEPHANE DE ASIS, stonecutter in Haute Provence, who was my associate during my formative years;

PROFESSORS GEORGE BUNKER (the owner) and LOUIS FREY (my neighbour), both now deceased, who allowed me to live and work at the Maison du Rocher in the Bibemus stone quarry from 1980 onward, and to the City of Aix-en-Provence, who, after receiving the property as a legacy, allowed me to continue my work and residency there;

LES COMPAGNONS DU DEVOIR DU TOUR DE FRANCE, for their part in maintaining a centuries old manual craft, and for having allowed me to participate in several of their classes and workshops in Alsace in 1980.

Foreword

Although this book is about architecture and about building, it is above all a book about a traditional hand craft, that of working stone. My first goal is to add to the reader's knowledge of traditional (pre-industrial) architecture, particularly that of Europe; to this end you have the 227 photos of Part 1, which I hope will delight and inspire you. My second is to reveal to you something about the crafts of working with stone (stone-masonry, and especially, stone-cutting); perhaps this book will de-mystify these for some people, who will realize that they are capable of doing such work, either professionally or for building their own houses; for others, it will at the least allow them to better understand the work that went into the buildings which are our heritage, and to appreciate the crafts which gave rise to them and which can still be practised today.

Part 1, while providing photo documentation on all the different degrees of simplicity or refinement possible in building with stone, as well as a historical overview of European architecture, also gives much insight into many practical aspects of building which a builder quickly discovers, but which an art historian might not have considered. Part 2 concentrates on the methods of executing the work.

My lengthy residence in Europe, and particularly, in the south of France, has determined the framework for this book, which concentrates on the regions I know best, and where I have much travelled and taken many photos. Although stonecutting is certainly not limited to Europe – many other civilizations, at many different ages, have produced beautiful and often equally ornate works – there is in Europe a tradition extending almost continuously through over 2000 years, with surviving examples of all degrees of simplicity through to refinement; sufficient matter in any case for understanding the techniques and skills that make up the stonecutter's craft.

Whether you approach this book as a traveller, as a student of art history, as an architect, or as a builder, we hope you will find means and inspiration in these pages.

David Campbell
Aix-en-Provence
January 8, 2010

www.architrad-books.com

Other Schiffer Books By The Author:
Wood in Traditional Architecture. ISBN: 9780764335815. $45.00

Other Schiffer Books on Related Subjects:
Colonial Architecture: Early Examples from the First State. George Fletcher Bennett Foreword by Bernie Herman. ISBN: 0764325108. $29.95
Early Domestic Architecture of Pennsylvania. Eleanor Raymond, Introduction by R. Brognard Okie. ISBN: 0764325906. $29.95
German Architecture in America. Irwin Richman. ISBN: 0764318004. $49.95
Half-Timber Architecture. Tina Skinner. ISBN: 9780764326677. $39.95
Shaker Architecture. Herbert Schiffer. ISBN: 0887401538. $24.95
Spanish Revival Architecture. Jerry "S. F." Cook III, Tina Skinner. ISBN: 0764323091. $49.95

Cover and book designed by: Bruce Waters
Type set in DeVinne BT & BT/Zurich BT

ISBN: 978-0-7643-3614-0
Printed in China

Schiffer Books are available at special discounts for bulk purchases for sales promotions or premiums. Special editions, including personalized covers, corporate imprints, and excerpts can be created in large quantities for special needs. For more information contact the publisher:

Published by Schiffer Publishing Ltd.
4880 Lower Valley Road
Atglen, PA 19310
Phone: (610) 593-1777; Fax: (610) 593-2002
E-mail: Info@schifferbooks.com

For the largest selection of fine reference books on this and related subjects, please visit our web site at **www. schifferbooks.com**
We are always looking for people to write books on new and related subjects. If you have an idea for a book please contact us at the above address.

This book may be purchased from the publisher.
Include $5.00 for shipping.
Please try your bookstore first.
You may write for a free catalog.

In Europe, Schiffer books are distributed by
Bushwood Books
6 Marksbury Ave.
Kew Gardens
Surrey TW9 4JF England
Phone: 44 (0) 20 8392 8585; Fax: 44 (0) 20 8392 9876
E-mail: info@bushwoodbooks.co.uk
Website: www.bushwoodbooks.co.uk

Contents

PART
ONE

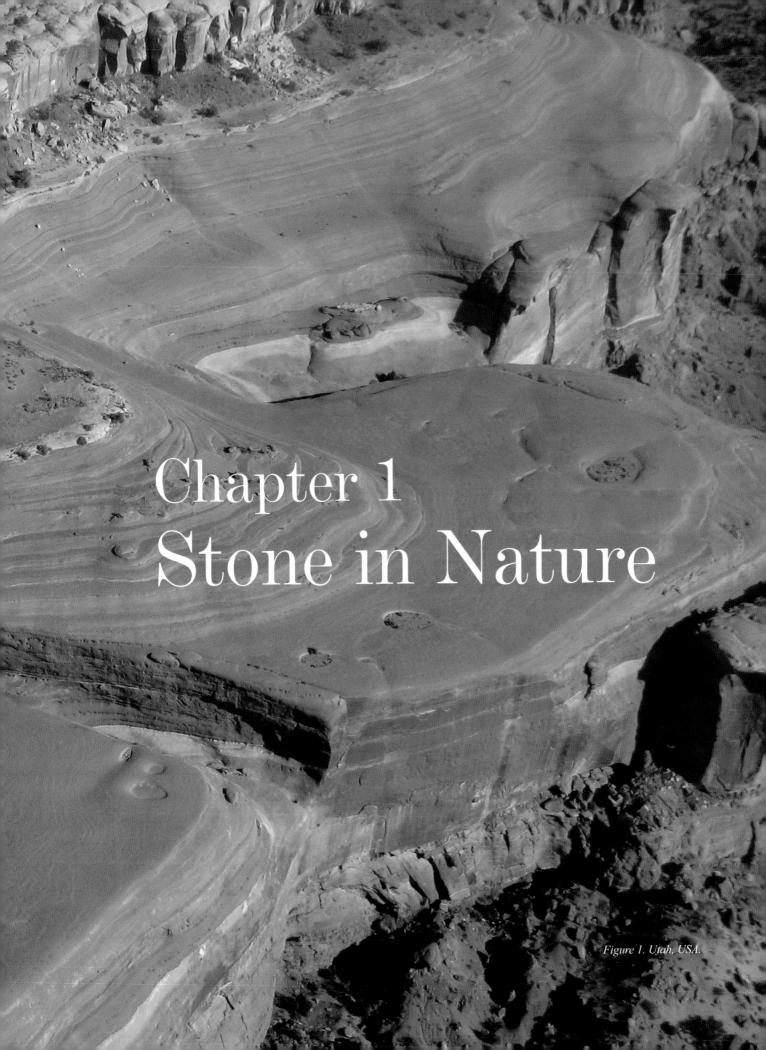

Chapter 1
Stone in Nature

Figure 1. Utah, USA.

Our planet, mostly composed of molten material in its interior, is covered on its surface by a relatively thin crust of rock, which permits the existence of its inhabitants. Part of this crust was previously liquefied in the intense heat of the Earth's interior. We can see, in the accompanying photos, how the rock was apparently flowing before solidifying on approaching the cooler surface.

The lowest-lying areas were progressively covered with water, forming oceans; even in the higher-lying areas, hollows would often fill with water to form lakes or swamps. The sediments carried by rivers and deposited on their adjacent plains allowed plants and trees to take root and find nourishment during their life cycle, their subsequent decomposition further adding to and enriching the layer of "earth" on the planet of the same name.

Each of these materials has been used by the human race, since its appearance on Earth, for the construction of its shelters. An account of the use of wood and other vegetal material is given in the book "**WOOD in Traditional Architecture**", and a future volume will deal with earth; this volume will consider particularly the use of STONE.

Figures 2-4. The 30,000 Islands, Georgian Bay, Ontario, Canada.

8

Figure 6. Colorado, USA.

Figure 7. Valais, Switzerland.

Figure 5. Edge of the Can (Plateau) de l'Hospitalet, Cévennes Mountains, France.

As most of the Earth's surface is covered with water, sand, forests, or other plants growing in soil, there are relatively few areas where stone is visible. Sometimes, such places can be used as **quarries**, sources of good building stones. Cliffs are natural quarries, because they present surfaces where the rock is exposed to the wearing forces of nature and gravity, and those rocks which break off from the surface will accumulate, over time, at the foot of the cliff.

Figure 8. Isle of Skye, Scotland.

11

Figure 9. The quarry of Bibemus, a deposit of soft yellow limestone just outside Aix-en-Provence, France. The quarry was exploited for the construction of a large part of the city in the seventeenth and eighteenth centuries.

Figure 10. A partly underground quarry in Lacoste, Provence, France, cut into a deposit of soft white limestone.

As well as such easily exploitable places, too few to supply all the necessary building materials as societies developed, man has throughout history sought out other sites where building stones could be removed, even if considerable effort was necessary. Often, a cliff face would be exploited, blocs of stone being cut or broken off through a depth of 20-50 cm, from the top of the cliff to its base, and the process repeated as long as usable stone, and the demand for it, lasted – often during centuries, for a good-sized quarry.

Where natural cliffs did not exist, quarrymen were sometimes able to dig galleries into a usable mass of solid stone, thus creating rock faces which could be exploited. Blocks can be cut or broken off of the mass in one of the following ways, depending on the type of the stone:

Figure 11. A sandstone cliff whose base has been exploited as a quarry. Canton of Bern, Switzerland.

13

Hard Limestone is generally found in horizontal strata, unless geological stresses have inclined the entire deposit. Different calcium-containing substances, primarily the shells of crustaceous sea creatures, deposited at different periods throughout time, combine with different sediments. The percolation of water bearing calcium particles through the mass leads to the cementing, over time, of all the components into a solid mass of rock. Certain strata may be of a softer material, such as clay, which will leave a fault line. These can be opened with an iron pry bar or with wedges. The stone thus opened horizontally will break somewhere in the vertical plane also; smaller stones are thus broken off of the mass. If the blocks obtained are still too big to be used conveniently, they can be further broken up with a sledgehammer. The stone is placed so that the line along which the mason or quarryman intends it to break rests on the edge of another stone or of an iron bar. Otherwise, if the stone is fairly long, it can be placed in such a way that its two ends are supported but its middle is not, in which case it can be broken in two with by a blow to the middle.

If the stone is very thick (more than about 15 cm / 6 in.), it is probably necessary to persist by repeatedly striking the same spot until the rock splits. If the stone is very wide, it will also be necessary to strike repeatedly at different points along a line across its width. Beyond a certain thickness, variable for each case but generally around 20 to 30 cm (8 to 12 in.), the stone cannot be broken by human strength, and will first have to be re-split along a horizontal fault line to give thinner stones.

Figures 13-14. Stephane de Asis, stonecutter in Upper Provence, using the sledgehammer to break a stone.

Figure 15. This sledgehammer has a slight concavity in its end. The user strikes the stone with one of the two edges separated by the concavity. The tool shown in the accompanying photos has one pointed end, but this is not necessarily the case; usually both ends are rectangular.

Shale is also found in strata, or layers, but here the strata are usually thinner and less tightly bound than in most limestones, so it is easy to separate them. When the strata are very thin (less than 5 cm), much care must be taken in separating them to avoid their breaking up into unusable pieces, but when this operation is done well, the quarryman can produce great quantities of thin flat stones usable for roofing.

Figure 16. Shale outcropping in the Cévennes Mountains, France.

Granite is a very hard material, formed of magma in the center of the earth, and solidified upon approaching the surface. Nonetheless, and in spite of its reputation for durability, it does erode over the centuries and the millenniums when exposed. As it tends to split neatly along fault lines under geological stresses, it is often found naturally in large blocks with flat surfaces. But exposed on hilltops (as here, on the Mont Lozère) or in riverbeds, it will become rounded due to wind and water erosion. Blocks which are too big to be manipulated can be split up, but the mason or quarryman must use his acquired judgment to predict where the block can best be split, as the strata are not as clearly seen as in shale or limestone. He will then bore a series of holes along the anticipated fault line (a job once done by repeatedly striking and rotating a hand drill). He will then hammer iron wedges into the holes, and will drive them in, bit by bit, one after the other, repeating the series of blows until the stone finishes by splitting along the line of wedges.

Figure 17.

Figure 18. The grooves left on the surface of the rock face after extraction of the stone are the marks of the pickax used to separate the blocks from the mass. The observer can see that the stone has been taken out in layers cut to about 25 cm (10 inches) high.

Soft limestone. Like the hard limestones described above, soft limestones are also deposited, during their formation, as layers of different component materials, including especially calcium from different types of sea-shells. These strata, however, are sometimes not easy to distinguish for the untrained eye. Contrary to hard stones, the soft stones do not break well when struck, as their particles tend rather to be crushed by the hammer blows, which are thus cushioned. To separate the blocks from the mass when exploiting the faces of a quarry (see figures 9 and 10, pp 12 and 13, as well as figure 18 above), grooves are cut, and progressively deepened, with a pickaxe, both behind and on the sides. The block can then be detached from the mass by splitting it off, along a horizontal fault line, with wedges, as described above, or with a heavy pry-bar. To further split up a big block once it has been detached, a combination of methods works best; first, a groove is chiselled out on the upper three sides (this will enable the quarryman to split the block precisely where he wants); then the block is split by driving in wedges inserted at different points along the grooves.

Figure 19. The groove can be cut with the stone ax if the stone is soft enough; otherwise, this is done with a chisel.

Figures 20-21. When the chisels driven into the groove are struck repeatedly, the block will finish by splitting.

21

Sandstone is composed of grains of sand compacted and hardened naturally over thousands of years. It is very abrasive, and quickly wears away metal tools. For this reason, it is also used to make whetstones for sharpening these same tools. It is usually a fairly hard stone, although some deposits can be so loosely bound that they disintegrate easily, and cannot be used for construction.

Those quarries which were exploited with hand tools bear the marks of the pickaxes used to separate the blocks from the cliff face, in the same manner as do the soft limestone quarries. And in the same way, the blocks are split along horizontal veins with wedges to complete the extraction.

Figures 22-25. Sandstone cliffs in Switzerland, some of which were exploited to provide the stone to build the cities of Bern and Freiburg, as well as many villages in these cantons.

Sandstone comes in a variety of colors: red, pink, orange, yellow, beige, grey, chestnut, bordeaux, and probably others as well; and some deposits present veins of different hues.

In France, the largest deposits are found in the Vosges Mountains and are predominently red or pink, or beige. Most of Alsace is built of stone from these numerous quarries. But small deposits, often very local, can be found in many places - amongst others, Villecomtale, in Rouergue (Aveyron), Clairvaux, also in Rouergue, and Collonges la Rouge, in Corrèze. It is surprising to come across these villages with their sophisticated architecture of red stone after having driven many miles through ajacent countryside bearing no resemblance to these special geological pockets.

Marble is a kind of limestone which has been metamorphosed into a hard stone under intense pressure. The layers thus hardened were generally those which were at one time at the bottom of a very thick load of sedimentary rock; some of these layers may later reappear at the earth's surface due to geological upheavals.

Under the name "marble" are sometimes classified the **breccia**, conglomerates of different kinds of stone, often in pebble form, cemented together by the hardening of the sediments which bind the whole. These can be considered marble by stonecutters, as they can be polished, but they are not real marble by geologists' classification.

Two different methods of extraction were used in the quarry shown here, on the slopes of the Montagne Sainte Victoire, in Provence, which produced a *breccia* conglomerate: some of the blocks have been extracted by cutting them out with a pickax; others have been sawed. In this case, the saw was a very long cable, which was driven by a motor, as the quarry was exploited until into the 20th century. The cable wore away, rather than cut, a groove into the stone. A stream of water was continually passed on the surface where the cable worked the stone, cooling it while also increasing the abrasiveness. Even in classical times, marble was sawed, but with a saw blade without teeth, handled by two men. Sand or another abrasive powder was thrown continually under the blade. Slowly, the abrasion would wear away a cut in the stone, and the process was continued until the block was separated from the mass.

Figure 26. Some of the remaining rock faces of a conglomerate marble (breccia) quarry, in Provence, France. The one in the foreground remains after extraction by sawing; that in the middle ground shows the oblique marks of pickax work.

Figure 27. Surface worked with a pickax.

Figure 28. Sawed surface partly polished by the wear of the sawing cable. A smoother and brighter polish can be obtained by sanding with abrasive powders; several passages can be made with increasingly fine powders until the desired finish is obtained.

Marble was the material which the ancient Greeks preferred for temples and public buildings, and several quarries were exploited in the Aegean islands to this end. Marble was also very much in fashion in Imperial Rome several centuries later, where it was used in thin plaques as a veneer to cover walls made of earth and clay or of irregular fieldstone set in a bed of mortar. The Romans liked this material, whose principal characteristics are its varied colors – varied even within the same piece – and its capacity to be polished to a smooth and even shiny surface. The Emperor Augustus boasted of having "found a Rome of clay" and having "left a Rome of marble" by his building programs. It would be more precise, though, to say that he left a Rome of clay covered with a veneer of marble.

Figure 29. Saw cut separating a large block from the mass; big iron wedges have been placed under the block (at the left) to prevent its settling in this direction and blocking the movement of the cable in the groove.

Figure 30. Blocks taken from the mass, awaiting transport down to the valley. (They have been waiting for a century now.)

Figure 31. Walls of granite, Mont Lozère, France.

Chapter 2
Masonry

IN THE BEGINNING...

Figure 32.

Since time out of mind, humans and animals have used caves as dwellings. The primary necessity is to have a dry shelter, which the covered cavity provides; the second, in cold climates, is to remain (relatively) warm, which the thick rock walls permit. If the cave opening is blocked off, the rock walls will retain some of the heat produced inside. If a fire is maintained permanently, then, the cave will provide a relatively comfortable environment.

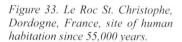

Figure 33. Le Roc St. Christophe, Dordogne, France, site of human habitation since 55,000 years.

Prehistoric man undoubtedly experimented with masonry by piling up rocks to close up a cave. As stones usually abound at the foot of cliffs, there would likely be an easily exploitable source of material near most caves. Over time, builders also saw that they could coat these walls with clay to prevent the passage of air between the stones; better still, the clay could be placed between the stones as they were set up, which also increased the stability of the piled-up rocks. As it was necessary to leave an entrance, doorways would have been created, with the ends of the stones all aligned more or less vertically. Such openings could be temporarily closed with animal skins, or with some other lightweight material, such as branches or interwoven reeds, easy to move aside.

Figures 34-35. Hypothetical reconstitution (after archaeological finds) of an oval collective dwelling, built about 2500 BCE by sedentary crop-growers in the Languedoc region of southern France. Musée de la Préhistoire, Quinson, France.

The builders of the time must have understood that these same masonry techniques could also be used to enclose a space under an overhanging cliff, or even on open ground. But it was not until the development of a sedentary way of life based on agriculture (in Europe, about 6000 BC) that these techniques came into general use, because as long as people remained nomadic, they were satisfied with more quickly and easily built shelters made of branches and covered with skins, leaves, bark, or reeds. (See *WOOD in Traditional Architecture*, by the same author.) But once the sedentary life increasingly motivated people to devote time and energy to building dwellings, which would be used for years and perhaps for generations, stone building became important to humanity. Timber and earth construction also became important; the favored material was usually whichever was the most plentiful in any given area.

From the beginnings of the agricultural era onwards, then, hamlets and villages increasingly appeared everywhere. In Europe, vestiges of dwellings made of stone over 5000 years ago have been discovered on the island of Minorca, on mainland Spain and Portugal, in the British Isles, and elsewhere*. In very poor regions, where the dwellings of the peasantry have evolved little through the ages, we can best get an idea of what these dwellings were like. Archaeologists studying the Neolithic site of Skara Brae in the Orkney Islands, Scotland, have made drawings reconstituting typical dwellings; the eighteenth century houses reconstituted on the isle of Lewis, another Scottish island char-

acterized by poor soil, short growing seasons, and lack of vegetation, closely resemble those sketches. A makeshift roof structure, composed of whatever wood was washed ashore, just barely covers the opening inside the walls, as these timbers – or whatever, because even material such as whale jaw-bones was used – were often not long enough to also cover the tops of the walls. Rainwater would consequently penetrate into the walls, which were covered only with sod and living grass, and would seep toward the outside due to the slope given the stones by the mason. Here it would drain away from the house due to the slope of the terrain. The walls can be plastered with clay on the inside.

Figure 36. Gearrannan Blackhouse Village: reconstitutions of eighteenth century peasant houses, Isle of Lewis, Scotland.

Figure 37. Callanish, Isle of Lewis, Scotland.

Figure 38. The Ring of Brodgar, Orkney Islands, Scotland.

A common practice at this period was the construction of stone funeral chambers; a chamber, and sometimes also a lengthy passageway, was made with very large and heavy slabs set on edge, which supported other slabs set horizontally on top of these, like a ceiling. The ensemble was often covered up with earth and/or stones to create a mound. Such structures are called dolmens (the covered chamber), or barrows (the ensemble covered with earth and stone).

Certain communities*** also set up huge stones vertically, in circles or alignments. Although the purpose of these sites is unknown with certainty, most observers concur that they were of religious and ceremonial significance, and that some of their alignments were used to mark the solstices and other significant astronomical events purporting to changing tides and seasons.

Figures 39-40. The Anasazi, an Amerindian people, used these overhanging cliffs of pink sandstone and the abundance of nearby stone to build several villages in the area; here, the site of Mesa Verde, Colorado, USA.

DIFFERENT KINDS OF STONE AND THE RESULTING MASONRY

Traditional constructions using natural materials are almost always in harmony with their environment, as they spring from it. A good example are these villages of Amerindian peoples (the Anasazi) built in the shelter of overhanging cliffs of pink sandstone.

The appearance of a stone wall depends on a variety of factors determined by the geological conditions of its locality: do the stones break up neatly along well defined shear lines, leaving flat surfaces? Are they easy to break up into smaller stones? Soft enough to be shaped with a chisel? Easy to trim with blows from a hammer? Do they split up into slabs, or do irregularly shaped pieces with no flat surfaces break off from the mass? The stones which come from the same geological deposit will have these characteristics in common, which is what gives distinctive local masonry forms, aspects, and traditions. Some examples follow:

Figure 41. Cliffs and buildings of pink sandstone; site of Mesa Verde, Colorado, USA.

Figures 42-43. On the Mont Lozère, whereas the houses are almost always built using mortar, most stables and outbuildings use the "dry" technique (without mortar).

Figures 44-45.

Granite is broken up only with much effort (involving the drilling of many holes in a very hard substance, see p 19). For this reason, masons tended, in pre-industrial times, to use big stones rather than break them up further. (The drawback, of course, is that they are harder to manipulate and put into place, but apparently, many builders considered this to be the lesser problem.) And as this material is difficult to shape, due to its hardness, the stones were used much as they were when split off from the mass, with a minimum of reshaping —at least, where peasant houses were concerned, as here, on the Mont *Lozère. Small stones were used only when they could be found in a rock pile where nature had already done the work of breaking them up.

Figures 46-47. Storage sheds made of shale, Cévennes Mountains, France. Figure 47 is a clède, for curing chestnuts. The floor which would normally be between the ground and the upper story is replaced with a wire mesh, on top of which the chestnuts are piled; a slow burning, smoky fire is maintained on the ground floor throughout the three month curing process, and the chestnuts can thus be preserved for the entire year.

Shale breaks up easily into flat stones, which can be split further, or broken up with hammer blows into smaller elements. Consequently, walls made of shale are usually composed of small, flat stones, giving an overall impression of horizontality, even when the rows are completely irregular.

Figure 48. Storage shed in Rouergue, France.

Figure 49. Storage shed in the Cévennes Mountains.

The example in Figure 48 also shows how doors and windows can be installed in a stone wall by the incorporation of a wooden frame.

Figure 50. Farm outbuilding made of shale, Cévennes Mountains, France.

Walls can be made of any kind of stone which doesn't fall apart while being handled, or break when dropped from (about) thigh level. All shapes of stones are also usable, but the flatter the stones, the quicker and easier it is to set them up into a stable wall. Irregular stones can of course be used, but more time must be taken to assemble them, like a jigsaw puzzle.

Figure 51. Outbuilding made of hard limestone; Spain (Province of Burgos).

Even rounded river stones are usable, but these depend greatly on a binding mortar for their stability. A well-built wall does not depend on mortar for its cohesion; before the era of industrial cement, walls were either set up "dry" (without mortar), or else using a clay, or a sand and lime, mortar. (See the last part of this chapter for a description of lime mortar making.) The mortar was merely a filler between the stones, and did not harden as much as modern cements. Nonetheless, on drying, it set solidly enough to block any movement of the individual stones, while still retaining a slight flexibility, enabling the wall to adjust to small settling movements without the mortar cracking. The mortar, which can be as thick or as fluid as the mason wishes, will partly be squeezed out from under the stone which the mason is setting, to flow into and fill any adjacent spaces. By thickening the mortar, the mason gives more support to the stones he sets; still, if he feels that a stone is not stable, he can block it with a shim, a smaller stone. The most useful shims are wedge-shaped, enabling the mason to slide them in further or less, to lift or incline the supported stone according to the need. The stone being set should not rock, once in place, if a light pressure is applied anywhere around its edges. When blocking has been placed between an inner and an outer wall (this will be explained further on in this chapter), the top of the wall can be walked on (gently) without dislodging any stones once the mortar has partly set, a few hours later.

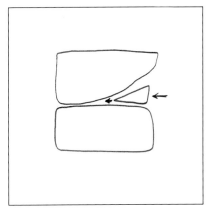

Figures 52-54.

MASONRY WITH FLAT STONES

The mason begins each level by setting the cornerstones, both at the corners of the building and at the door and window openings. As these right-angled stones are the most difficult ones to find in any given rock pile, it is best not to further complicate the task by also having to take into consideration whether they are the right length to fit into the adjoining masonry ; for this reason, the adjacent masonry is done afterwards, and is adjusted to the already set corners. The mason will set aside the suitable corner stones as he discovers them in his rock pile, and reserve them for this function.

Each joint of the row already in place should be covered by a stone of the row on top of it; this avoids a weak line in the wall where a vertical joint continues through several layers of masonry. Often, when the mason is dealing with flat or nearly flat stones, each level will be made up of stones of the same height, but the height of any given level will probably differ from that of most of the others. This is preferable, moreover, as it avoids the visual monotony of complete uniformity. To build with parallel, horizontal levels, the stones used must have their top and bottom surfaces parallel. When this is not the case, the mason will not be able to avoid jumps in the levels, but he nonetheless tries to maintain an overall impression of horizontality.

MASONRY WITH IRREGULAR STONES

Adopting the following system can simplify masonry with irregular stones. In the bottom row, set abutting stones in such a way that a concavity is formed where they join. When setting the rows above, choose each stone to have a convexity in its bottom surface which will fit in fairly well into a concavity of the row beneath (1). Any remaining gaps can be filled with appropriately chosen stones (2).

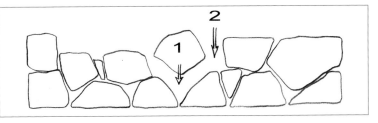

The mason will use small stones as shims as required to stabilize the stones he is setting

Other factors on which a wall's stability depends are its width (thickness), and the way in which the stones are fitted together.

The width: The wider the base, the more stable the wall, and thus, the higher it can be built. Walls which are made to last will consequently have a double thickness of stones, one presenting a fairly flat surface on the outside of the wall, and the other, on the inside. (See the sketch BELOW.) Between the two is set a fill of rubble stones, which have no good surfaces and are thus not useful in the wall's faces.

Overlapping the stones: A continuous vertical joint is to be avoided, as explained in the above schema. In building the wall's face, then, the stones to be set are chosen to have, among other criteria, lengths allowing them to overlap the vertical joints of the level below.

This general rule (which can be transgressed occasionally) applies especially to the faces of the wall (see the sketch of the elevation), but also, to a lesser extent, to the thickness of the wall (see the sketch of the CROSS SECTION, BELOW).

Masonry books often instruct apprentice masons to occasionally place a stone through the entire thickness of the wall, as a binder, as at **A**, in figure 55. Ideally, this is a good practice, but stones of precisely the dimensions required for this are very hard to find. If the mason finds nothing suitable in his rock pile, he can nonetheless ensure sufficient cohesion by occasionally overlapping the inside ends of the inner and outer walls, as at **B** and **Y**. If the end of a stone is overlapped both above and below, moreover, as with **C** between **X** and **Y**, or **Y** between **C** and **B**, the binding effect is even better. But the case of figure 56 should be avoided.

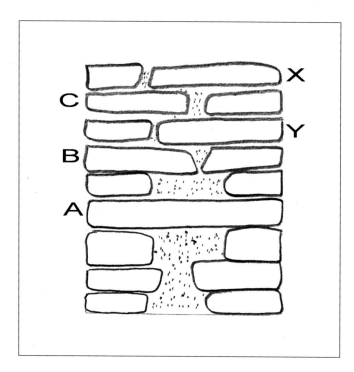

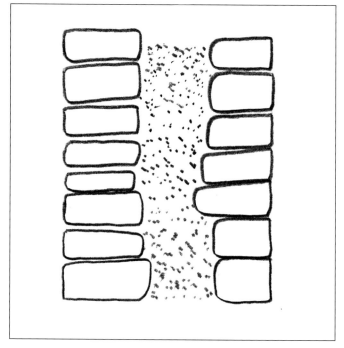

Figures 55-56.

Tieing one wall in with another is also of great importance to the stability of the building. On the inside corner, one wall penetrates the other by overlapping the corner stones in alternating courses; on the outside, the stones are chosen to alternate short sides and long sides, thus avoiding a prolonged vertical joint over several courses.

Figure 57.

Figure 58. Farm buildings in Upper Provence. The one at the far left must have been added on at a later date, because it has simply been put up next to the adjacent building; had the two been built at the same time, the two walls would have been interlocked, and there would be no long vertical joint at their junction. But although such construction does not offer the maximum possible resistance to stress, it has nonetheless held up for (about) two hundred years, and is still in good condition.

Figure 59.

LIME and OTHER MORTARS

The first mortar was undoubtedly a mixture of earth and clay. Because these materials exist in nature and need no transformation other than the addition of water, they were available to man from the beginning of his time on earth. Clay, a sticky substance, acts as a binder for earth and sandy material, which could not hold together without it. It does not, though, resist water, and is quickly washed away if exposed. Lime, on the other hand, does not have this disadvantage, but its production requires considerable means, beyond those or prehistoric or early agricultural societies, and its use did not become generalized until the time of the Roman Empire.

Lime was produced by baking limestone in a large oven constructed for this purpose. The firing process, at 800 to 1100 degrees C, lasted three full days or more, during which the fire was maintained in the lower portion of the oven, while the lime-containing material was piled above. The subsequent desiccation of the limestone produced **"quicklime"**. After removal from the oven, this substance, in stone-like pieces, can be transported to be sold.

At the building site, the quicklime is rehydrated by the addition of water. The reaction is quite violent, with corrosive material boiling and bubbling and sometimes being splattered about, so keep your distance if you do this.

When just the right amount of water has been added, the quicklime will disintegrate, after reaction, into a powder, which can be stored in a dry place; with a greater quantity of water, it will remain in the form of a paste, which can be kept as long as its surface remains covered with water. (This is only the case if the original stones do not contain a high proportion of clay, which would produce a "hydraulic lime", which hardens in the presence of water.) Whether in powder or in paste form, the resulting product is **"slaked lime"**, usually simply called **"lime"**. To make a mortar (also called **"lime"**), the slaked lime will act as a binder when added to an aggregate. The best aggregate is fine river sand, but a variety of aggregates, as well as the proportions in which they are mixed, is possible, according to the intended use. The peasant who could not obtain sand might mix lime with earth, often very parsimoniously. And the presence of large grains or even pebbles in the mortar is not a problem as long as the mason does not intend to make very thin joints in his masonry, or smooth the finish coat of rendering.

Depending on the purity of the original limestone, the resulting lime will be more or less pure, and its purity, as well as the use to which it will be put, will determine the proportions of lime to sand. This can vary, a coat of rendering requiring a higher dosage of lime than, say, the stone infill in a masonry wall. But to give a rough idea, the proportions will be approximately one part lime to two of sand for a rendering, falling to about one to five for work needing little cohesion.

Water is added, and a mortar sufficiently thick to be handled with a trowel is made. When this is used to set stone, it will dry and progressively absorb carbon dioxide from the air. Combined with calcium carbonate, the principal component of the lime, the mortar will harden. Apart from its use as a mortar, slaked lime was traditionally used pure, diluted with water but without the addition of any aggregate, as **whitewash** (for painting), or for filling very fine joints between precisely cut stones. (See Chapter 10, **Setting up an Arch**.)

42

As lime had a not negligible cost, it was not wasted by the poor. Peasants generally didn't use it when making outbuildings, reserving it rather for their houses. Sometimes, only those walls exposed to the prevailing rains would be rendered. In the towns, the lower quality masonries (those of rough, unshaped, stone) were generally rendered over; only those walls of cut stone or elements such as door and window frames would be left visible.

Figures 60-61.

Certain regions – usually those which were lacking a kind of stone which was easy to work and made handsome walls – developed a tradition of lime rendering, which has marked their appearance. Some of these raised the decoration of rendered walls to an art form, especially during the baroque period; see the photos THIS DOUBLE PAGE of houses in the Engadina Valley, canton Graubunden, in Switzerland, as well as those of the Austrian Tyrol.

Figures 62-65.

44

45

Figure 66. This photo shows a vaulted bread oven attached to (and opening onto the inside of) a farmhouse in the Cévennes Mountains. The eaves are made of slabs of granite, which is not a stone that can be finely split; hence the thickness and irregularity of these pieces, undoubtedly nonetheless the thinnest the mason could find. Used on the eaves, they rest on the wall, which can support them, and they help resist the outward push of the vault. To continue the roof toward its peak, though, smaller, thinner pieces of shale have been used.

ROOFS

Wherever stones are found that can be split into flat, thin slabs (generally, under 4 cm), these can be used for covering roofs. Since this is an attribute of local geological conditions, the architecture of certain areas is consequently characterized by certain types of roofs. Set atop vaults, roofing stones are usually set with mortar, but on roofs with a timber structure, they can be nailed onto a sheathing of boards; a hole for passing the nail will be punched through the stone with a pointed tool. Before iron nails became plentiful (mid to late 19th century), wooden dowels were often used.

Figures 67-68. Roofs of thick (2-3 cm) shale.

Figure 67. On the Mont Lozère, France.

Figure 68. Aveyron, France.

Figures 069-072. All photos Aveyron, France.

Shale is one kind of stone which is easily split into flat pieces; depending on the local variety, these may be as fine as half a centimeter (in which case it is *slate*). But even if its average thickness is about two cm, as on this double page, it can be trimmed to the fish-scale shape characteristic of certain regions. In areas producing shale or slate roofing stones, trimming and setting these gave rise to two specialized trades: roofers, and slaters.

The eaves are usually made with the biggest stones, which are trimmed to present a straight outer edge.

Figure 072.

Figures 73-75. The rooftops of Conques, in the Aveyron, southwest France.

A very particular way of setting roof stones is found in certain regions, such as in Dordogne (south-west France; LEFT and FACING PAGE). Here, small pieces of limestone are commonly found in the fields and rock outcroppings. To be able to use these, the local builders covered rafters with wooden battens spaced just slightly further apart than the stones are thick, and the stones' ends are stuck between two battens. The stones, irregular in length (and all other dimensions as well), are pushed in as far as necessary so that the outside ends are aligned in courses. Here again the load is very great, so the roof structure must be very resistant.

Figure 74.

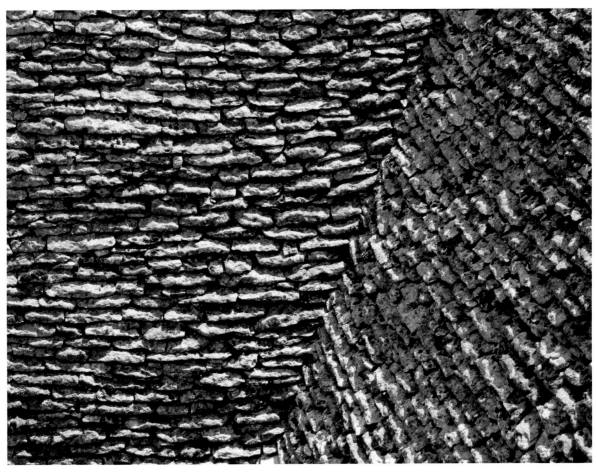

Figure 75.

51

Figure 76.

In certain parts of Haute Provence (here, near Forcalquier), the local limestone can be split into large flat slabs. Pieces 3 to 5 cm thick are used locally as roofing material. These stones tend to break if trimming is attempted, so they are used in the shape in which they come, and are set without a pattern. Although this appears haphazard, it requires much attention and experience, for each piece must shed its water onto another piece, and the way in which the water will run off is not obvious.

NOTES for this chapter

*Some archaeological sites where dwellings or fortifications made of stone have been unearthed are:

Las Navetas de Tudons (island of Minorca, Spain)
Los Millares (south-east Spain)
Zambujal (Portugal)
Chyauster (Cornwall, England)
Chun castle (Cornwall, England)
Dun Aonghasa (Isle of Aran, Ireland)
Dun carloway (Isle de Lewis, Scotland)
Skara Brae, (Orkney Islands, Scotland, where there are numerous other sites as well)
Losa (Sardinia, Italy)

** Some sites where vestiges of alignments or circles of standing stones are visible include:

Carnac (Brittany, France)
Stonehenge (Amesbury, Wiltshire, England)
Avebury (Wiltshire, England)
The Hurlers (Cornwall, England)
Dartmoor (many sites) (Devon, England)
Castlerigg (Cumbria, England)
Callanish (Isle of Lewis, Scotland)
Ring of Brodgar (Orkney Islands, Scotland)
Filitosa (Corsica, France)

This list is far from being exhaustive, naming only the most widely known; such sites are numerous in Brittany and in the British Isles.

***A notable exception is Roman concrete. Instead of sand, a volcanic powder called *pozzolan*, found nearby, was mixed with lime, and hardened into a very solid mass. This concrete was very important in the development of Roman architecture (see the note at the end of CH 5), but as the pozzolan deposits were very limited geographically, the techniques which it allowed could not be generalized to other localities.

****Ruins from the classical Greek period show that the Greeks and their colonies built their major monuments with solid walls, without infill. Either one very large block occupied the entire width of the wall, its ends being visible on both the inside and the outside faces; or, if several stones were assembled, these were set with the stones abutting one another, without any space for infill between them. Neither was mortar used; the blocks were held together with large metal pins shaped like staples. These were sealed with molten lead in holes cut into the stones for this purpose.

Figure 77. Ávila, Spain.

CHAPTER 3
CUT STONE

Cut Stone

Prehistoric man knew how to shape silex, which he *"knapped"*, or struck in a very precise way so as to break off thin flakes with a sharp edge. These were used to make many sorts of cutting tools; scrapers, knives, axes, hatchets, and adzes, amongst others. The idea of the *"shapeability"* of stone was thus acquired very early in time, and prehistoric man was undoubtedly capable of breaking off excess material when it was necessary to reduce a building stone in size for a better fit, or for the rudimentary dressing of a face.

As metallurgy became known to man (from about 3500 BC in the Middle East, and about 2000 BC in Europe), metal tools became common, and these enabled a very precise shaping of the stone. We know that some very old civilizations – Egypt, and also Persia - built temples and/or palaces out of cut stone, even before the Greeks and the Romans of the classical period. It is impossible to trace a linear development, though, because once the techniques were developed (very early, as we have seen), their use in any society depended mostly on the wealth of the persons concerned, the gap between the palaces of the rulers and the rudimentary houses of the peasantry being as great in ancient Egypt as it was under Louis XIV. So although I will explain how stone-working techniques varied in complexity, the techniques cannot necessarily be associated with a place or time - in contrast with the forms, which can be.

Rudimentary door and window openings

Door and window openings have always required particular attention from the mason. Even for the simplest of openings, he has to find stones with two faces at right angles [or almost] for the sides of the openings (the **jambs**), as well as for the corners of the building. As indicated in the preceding chapter, stones of this type being relatively scarce, the mason will set those he finds aside for this purpose, and not waste them in the middle of a wall, where the right-angle face will not be visible. When he does use them for the jambs, he must be as careful about the vertical alignment of the inside faces as about that of the façade.

Figures 78-79. Hypothetical reconstitution (after archaeological finds) of dwellings built about 2500 BCE by sedentary crop-growers in the Languedoc region of southern France. Musée de la Préhistoire, Quinson, France.

Figure 80. **Rabbet** *(right-angled indentation) in a granite doorway; Mont Lozère. Through the opening and across the courtyard can be seen the outside of a door closed against a similar doorframe.*

As societies developed and people improved their conditions of material comfort, they sought ways of better fixing their doors and window shutters to prevent the passage of cold air, as well as to protect them from being torn open by thieves or attackers. A solution was the inclusion of a **rabbet** (a right-angled indentation), into which the door or shutter fitted and closed tightly against, protecting its edges at the same time.

The rabbets could be created by adding an additional thickness of stones, offset by 4 or 5 cm in relation to the outside (façade) stones. But if this were to be done at each course, there would be a **sabercut** (continuous vertical joint), which could result in the outside door frame pulling away from the inside one under certain stresses. It became common practice, then, where the stone was not difficult to shape, to cut the rabbet directly into the stones making up the jambs, at least in alternate courses. The opening would consequently be built with that quality of stone which was the easiest to shape of the varieties available, even if this differed in appearance from the stone used for the walls.

Figure 81. Doorway made of shaped sandstone in a wall of shale. Cévennes Mountains, France.

Figures 82-84. Simple door and window openings of cut granite; Mont Lozère.

Figure 85. Door and window openings of cut limestone in a wall of rough stone of the same type; Village des Bories (open air museum), Gordes, Provence.

Figure 86. Granite; Mont Lozère.

*Figure 87. The village of Oppède le Vieux, in Provence. Both the walls and the openings are made of the same kind of stone, a soft limestone from nearby quarries. But whereas the walls were built using the **"découverte"** – that is, stones broken off the mass at its surface, where it is exposed to freezing and thawing – the stone for the openings is taken from a vein deeper down. As this was not exposed to the weather, it is of a better quality, and the blocks bigger and relatively free of flaws.*

The same is true for the house shown in Figure 85, which is only 15 km from this one, although its stone comes from a different quarry, these being numerous in the area. Stones similar in quality to those of the découverte are often found in the fields, moreover; and as they must be removed when the land is to be cultivated, this work (which is renewed with each plowing) can furnish an important quantity of building stones.

Once the procedure of using a different kind of stone for the openings is accepted, the possibilities for decorative work become unlimited, as we shall see on the following pages. But as these stones almost always come from a quarry from which a worker must extract them, and as they require considerable time and skill to shape (we will study the methods further on), the more cut stone went into a building, and the more complex its decoration, the costlier was the undertaking. Consequently, the peasant houses remained simple, the use of finely cut stone being limited, if used at all, to door and window openings without decoration, as can be seen in the three preceding double pages. Sometimes, though, even peasant houses will be made with stone that is roughly cut or partially cut, and often, variations in the standards of cutting can be seen in the same building.

Figure 88. In this simple house (the house of a quarry worker in the Bibemus quarry, in Provence), the outside faces of most of the stones have been cut roughly, to give a flat surface to the wall, but top, bottom, and side surfaces have rarely been retouched. No particular care has been taken with the door and window openings, which have simply been dressed with a coat of lime plaster, which also provides the rabbet for fitting the door (on the inside).

Figure 89. In this village in the Cévennes Mountains, the stones of the ruin in the middle ground are cut only on the outside faces and rarely on the other sides, as is also the case with the building on the facing page. The appearance of these two walls is very different, though, partly because of the color and texture of the stone (soft limestone at Bibemus, granite in the Cévennes), but mainly because of the ample use of mortar for the walls of the former.

Figure 90.

Figures 90-91. The house in the background in figure 89, though, is made entirely of cut stone, in contrast to the style of the ruin in the middle ground. But although the stones are set in horizontal courses, these have been adjusted only roughly. The wall in Figure 90, in the same village, shows greater unevenness still in the courses, but the stones have been cut to adjust to the irregularities of the adjacent stones, whereas in the wall to Figure 91 (still in the same village), each stone has been squared, and thus any one can be set next to any other of the same height.

Figure 91.

Figure 92. Sandstone roughly cut on the outside face and left unsquared. Castle in Alsace, France.

Figure 93. Roughly cut stones; here, the stones have (mostly) been squared to a greater extent than in the previous example, but the lack of precision still leads to very thick joints. Church in Toledo, Spain.

Figure 94. Precisely cut and squared sandstone wall; Church in Alsace.

Figure 95. (opposite) The grey granite for the window frame has been cut precisely, except for some of the outside edges, done roughly or not at all. The pinker stones, a different variety of granite, have been left uncut. As they bear no chisel marks, their flatness is probably due to their being split along natural fault lines during the quarrying. Ávila, Spain.

Figure 96. View of the apses of another Romanesque church, this one in Provence, France. It was obviously built with whatever was available, starting with the base rock, which forms the bottom third of the central apse. (Many sarcophagi (tombs) have been cut into the base rock all around the rear of the church; several of these can be seen in the photo.)

The major part of the walls are built using the découverte, *but in some places this have been squared up more than in others. Finally, the tower, which also houses the nave in the interior, is made of stones finely cut and adjusted. It is very hard to know if this was the original plan for the building, but this seems doubtful; the multitude of styles, and the juxtaposition of a second nef, show that whatever plan there originally may have been was modified, and the construction done in several stages.*

Figure 97. Apse of a Romanesque church, showing very precise standards of cutting, with tolerances of probably not more than 4 mm. Catalonia, Spain. (opposite)

Figure 98. St. Cirq la Popie, Quercy, France.

Figures 98-99. Finely worked window openings have been incorporated into walls made in very heterogeneous fashion, containing some portions made of fieldstone, and others made of roughly cut stone. Note how the cornerstones, (including the angles of the octagonal tower) are made of finely cut stone, increasing the stability of the masonry at these points of greatest stress.

Figure 99. Sarlat, Dordogne, France.

Figure 100. Zamora.

Figures 100-103. The entire facade of the buildings shown is made of finely cut and adjusted stone.

Figures 100-101. Spain: The door and window frames have been richly decorated in the exuberant plateresque style of the sixteenth century. (See also p 136.)

Figure 101. Salamanca.

Figures 102-103. Nuremburg, Germany.

Cutting stone allows the creation of almost any shape, which can greatly fluidify the architecture

Figures 104-105. Collanges-la-Rouge, Corrèze, France.

74

Figure 106. Biel/Bienne, Switzerland.

Figures 104-107. As you can see from these examples, a wide range of solutions, from fairly simple to extremely complicated, can be found for any architectural element. But even for the simplest, the slopes and angles must be calculated and reproduced precisely from stone to stone, and a cutting plan must be established beforehand so that the stones can be assembled with the proper continuity.

Figure 107. Lucerne, Switzerland.

Figure 108. Chillon Castle, Switzerland.

Figure 109. Pezenas, Languedoc region, France.

Even such a roughly cut (but finely adjusted) vault rib such as this (ABOVE LEFT), cut from a very hard limestone of its region, can fluidify the architecture; so much more is the case when the stone is easily shaped, such as in the two other photos, where a soft limestone is found in the vicinity. The springing stones (usually several, extending through several courses when they give rise to many ribs) are very complicated to trace, and were reserved for the most experienced stonecutters. Such pieces are often used as *master pieces* in the tests required for passing from journeyman to master in stonecutters' crafts guilds.

Figure 110. Vaulted ceiling of a church in the Dordogne area of France. See the section on Cross Vaults in Chapter 5.

Figure 111. A spiral staircase, viewed from below. In this case, the bottom surface of each step
has been cut to a curve to increase the spiralling, fan-like effect.

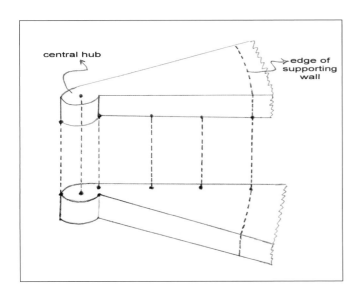

Figure 112a.

Figure 112. A view from above, showing the ruins of a tower housing
a spiral staircase. Bonaguil Castle, southwestern France.

Figure 113. Pezenas, Languedoc, France.

For any molding, curve, or pattern which must follow from one stone to another, as with the ribs of the vaults in the above photo, or the corbelled base of the tower in Figure 105 (bottom), or even for a simple arch, a template should be made of the cross section which is to be reproduced. This will be made real size, to the exact measurements of the figure to be cut. It will then be applied and traced onto both ends of each stone making up the series. When the stones are cut according to the profile, they will all follow without deviating from the pattern. (See The Stoneworker's Handbook, Chapters 10 and 11, and also Ch 6, Figure 223.)

The profile of the ribs in the vault above is shown here. (Figure 114)

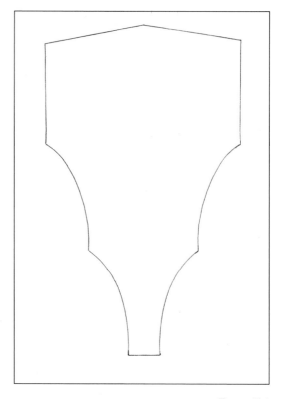

Figure 114.

78

A particular kind of rough-cutting is the **boss**, shown on this page. The edges of each stone's face are trimmed meticulously and are squared, but the face, on the inside of the chiselled edges, is left rough. Although time is saved by not dressing the whole surface, this gain is slight compared to the time, which must be taken for the preparation of each stone's periphery; the advantage of the boss is more a military concern. The stones are perfectly fitted, resulting in a strong construction, while leaving additional mass and volume for resistance against projectiles.

Figures 115-116. Landsberg castle, Alsace.

As the preceding pages have shown, the material stone, once its techniques have been mastered, provides enormous possibilities for the evolution and the refinement of architecture. In Europe, the period of the greatest evolution was undoubtedly the Middle Ages. As was the case with the carpenters, so the masons and stonecutters (whose crafts were not distinctly separated at the time) were also organized in crafts guilds, associations of men practising the same trade. These guilds, in which membership was practically obligatory for anyone wishing to work legally, determined the standards of work and the fees charged; regulated the training and conditions of employment of apprentices; and standardized their progression in the craft, ensuring that they passed through all the conventional steps of the apprenticeship, then of journeyman, before becoming masters, the masters alone having the right to open a workshop and practise commerce.

The decoration, and the architecture itself, as we will see (in Ch 5, Vaults) followed fashions which changed with time, and which are usually easily recognizable today. Some examples are shown here, and others will be seen in CH 6, *Architecture Through the Ages*.

Figure 117. Arcades forming an external gallery, Romanesque church of the twelfth century; Segovia, Spain.

Figure 118. Bishop's palace; Tarragona, Spain, thirteenth century.

Figure 119. Astrological clock in the south facade of the old City Hall, Prague, Czech Republic.

80

Figure 120. Window of a Romanesque church, twelfth century, Zamora, Spain.

Figure 121. Gothic turret built in the fourteenth century; east façade of the old City Hall of Prague, Czech Republic.

81

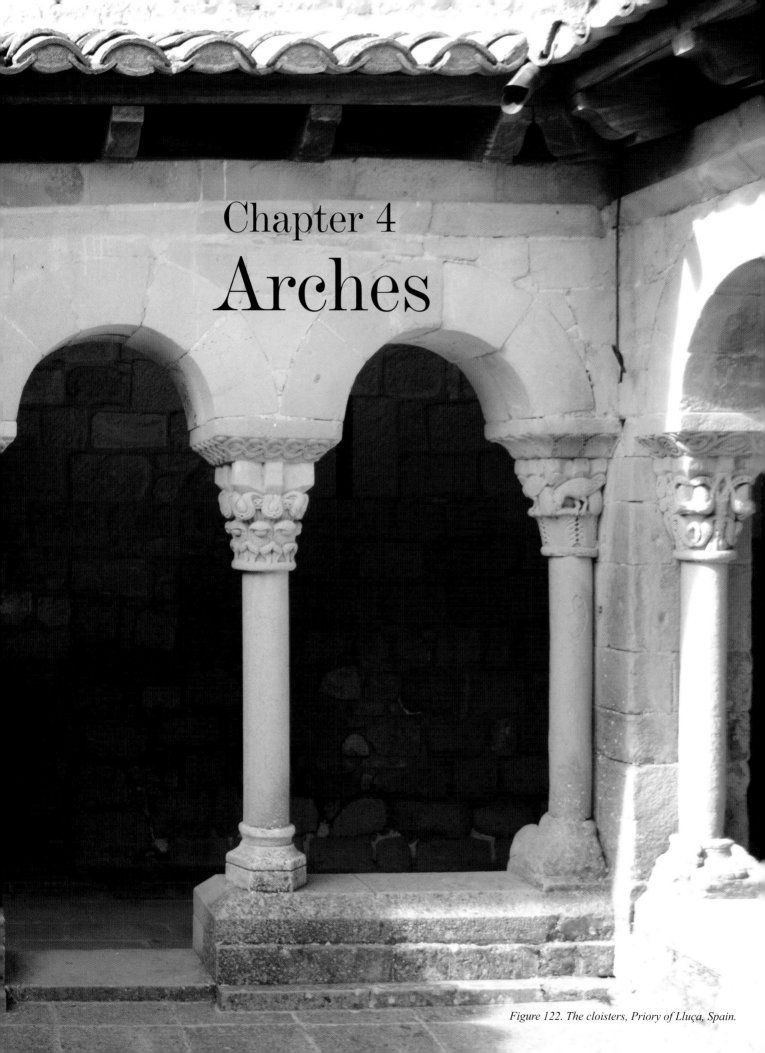

Chapter 4
Arches

Figure 122. The cloisters, Priory of Lluça, Spain.

Once a door or window opening has been created in a wall, it must be bridged at its top in order to continue to build above it. The simplest and easiest way of doing this is by setting a wooden lintel at the desired height, resting on the jambs at each side. It is, of course, possible to use a stone as the lintel, and this was done wherever wood was lacking. Wood is preferable, though, where it is available, for several reasons. For one, it can easily be cut into lengths greater than those in which stone is usually found, which is a great advantage to any builder wishing to create wide openings – as, for example, for a carriage entranceway.

Also, for the same thickness, wood will withstand much heavier loads in flexion (that is, weighing down on its middle,) than will stone. Stone is rarely useful for spanning more than one meter, and for this, it must be about 30 cm. (1 foot) thick. In addition, it must be longer than the opening spanned, resting on the jambs on each side by about 20 cm. As blocks of such dimensions are not readily available, nor easy to move, the reader can understand that this solution was not often used for spanning large openings. It was, nonetheless, the one chosen by the Greeks of classical times, who quarried enormous blocks for use as lintels in their temples. The result was impressive, although the effort required was correspondingly enormous.

The Romans used a more efficient system, which had in fact been used before them by the Assyrians in the Tigris and Euphrates Valleys (present-day Iraq), a region where neither rocks nor trees were abundant. Because of this, its inhabitants used unbaked bricks of earth as their usual building material, and they learned to assemble a series of these small elements in a self – supporting curve. This practice was taken up by the Romans, who applied it to stone. The arch enabled builders to replace huge lintels with a series of much smaller and more easily movable stones. These stones, which in theory are wider at the top than at the bottom*, are set up temporarily on a curved form while all the elements are being put in place, where they will wedge against one another so that they cannot fall once the support is removed – as long as there is also a blocking masonry along its sides to absorb the lateral thrusts. (See the following drawing.)

Figure 123. The elements of an arch are (theoretically) wider on the outside (top) of the curve than on its inside (bottom), and will thus wedge against one another and not fall.*

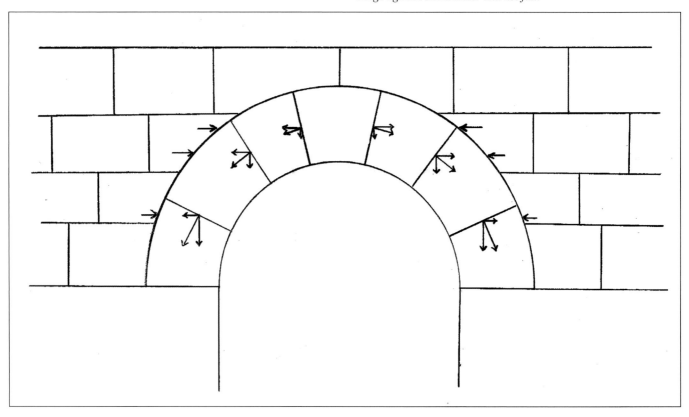

They force against one another at right angles to the surface where they are in contact, and this force can be decomposed into a horizontal (lateral) component as well as a vertical component. The total of the accumulated lateral forces must be resisted by an equal force, provided, in this case, by the masonry on each side of the arch. The vertical forces are transferred to the jambs, and through them to the ground.

Figure 124. Width of the opening: about 80 cm. Lintel made of pine; walls of hard limestone. Upper Provence.

Figure 125. Width of the opening: approx. 50 cm. Shale; Cévennes Mountains

Figure 126. Width of the opening: approx. 70 cm. at the narrower top part. Soft limestone, Provence. The building has apparently settled unevenly, resulting in the lintel's cracking, in spite of its thickness.

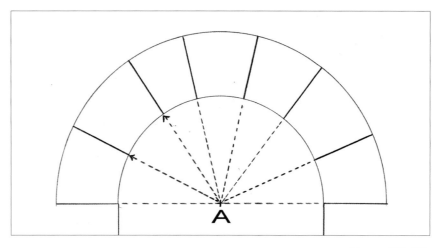

Figures 127-129.

The semicircular arch

The Romans habitually used the arch in semicircular form. This is subdivided into pieces whose joints all originate at A, the center of the circle. The circle's diameter will correspond to the distance between the jambs to be spanned.

Usually, the Romans divided each arch into an odd number of stones, all of equal dimensions. The keystone, which (unless it was meant to protrude or have some kind of decoration) was not in any way different from any of the other stones, was consequently perfectly centered. But at many other periods and places, such regularity was not a principle. In medieval masonry, for instance, the stonecutters usually tried to get the maximum possible usable volume out of any block. Thus, a stone cut out of a large block would not be shortened to make it conform in size to the others; indeed, there was no standard size to which it had to conform. Nor was the keystone necessarily centered.

The outside curve (the extrados) is cut as roughly, or as precisely, as are the edges of the stones in the surrounding masonry. Sometimes, it is simply sketched out by cutting the curve only to a depth of about 2 cm – just enough to leave a visible trait – while leaving the rest of the mass rough. This is especially the case when the walls, probably of rough stone, are to be plastered or rendered, leaving only the cut stone elements visible, as in Figure 128. When the entire extrados is cut, and fits into a wall of stones cut to the same precision, those that abut the arch will fit its contours perfectly. (See figures 129, 133, and 135 below).

It is also possible to add one or several rows of arches with moldings or sculpted motifs. This was moreover a common practice from Roman times onward for any buildings which were meant to be impressive. These supplementary arches are also cut to have their joints radiating from the center of the principal arch. These can be seen in the photo opposite.

Figure 128. Semicircular arches in an Alsatian village (France); the smaller door is the pedestrian entrance; the larger one allows the passage of carts and carriages into the courtyard.

Figure 129. Entranceway of a Romanesque church, Avilà, Spain.

The pointed arch

Another form of arch, much used during the Middle Ages (see Chapter 5, *VAULTS*, for an outline of its importance for the development of gothic architecture), is the pointed arch. As its name indicates this is not a continuous curve like the semicircular arch, but is made up of two curves, which meet at a pointed summit. Its joints radiate from two different centers, which are offset, symmetrically, from the central axis between the two jambs. Although the two curves are of the same diameter, the diameter can vary from one arch to another, and this possibility of variations gives rise to a number of different shapes, with curves more or less pronounced, and with their summits at different heights.

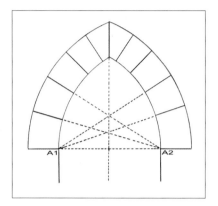

*Figure 130. **Equilateral:** this is a special (but common) case of the pointed arch, where the center points are situated precisely on the limits of the opening.*

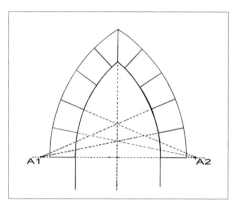

*Figure 131.**Higher arch, or lancet:** the center points are situated on the **outside** of the opening.*

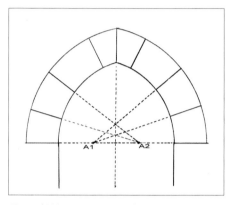

*Figure 132. **Lower arch:** the center points are situated on the **inside** of the opening.*

Figure 133. Low pointed arches; Villeneuve de Rouergue, France.

Figure 134. Pointed arch; gateway in the defensive walls of the city of Ávila, Spain.

Figure 135. Pointed arch; entrance to the Gothic cathedral of Nuremburg, Germany.

The keystone can be a single, centered, stone, or two stones can be assembled on either side of the central axis.

Other forms

The drawing at right (see Figure 132, p 88) suggests another form, which came to be much used in Renaissance architecture: the basket handle. As the springing of the low pointed arch gives an abrupt curve which may be perceived as being awkward (see Figure 133), architects and master builders experimenting with other forms found a way to smooth out this "fault" while still maintaining the arch's summit low. This is done by composing the arch of three curves; it thus has three centers; two aligned on the horizontal springing line, and the third one situated much lower, on the vertical axis between the two jambs. The form of this arch, in appearance an unbroken curve, resembles a basket handle, giving the arch its name. Some experimenting must be done, 'though, in the drawing stage, to determine the center points and the compass openings (radii) which will give a suitable curve when assembled together.

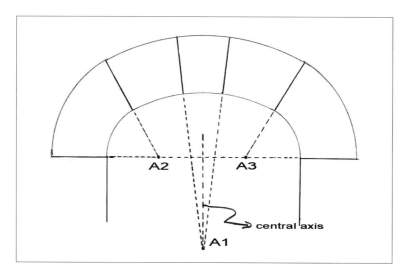

Figure 136.

Figure 137. Sarlat, Dordogne, France.

Figure 142. Pointed arc with trefoils (three lobes) and an archivolt in the form of an **accolade**, a style much favored in sixteenth century Venice and those Dalmatian cities under its influence. (See also pp 126 and 127.) This example is from Split, in what is now Croatia.

Figure 138. Basket-handle arches at the upper level; semi-circular at the street level. Main square of Zamora, Spain.

A variation of this form was much used in Moslem Persian architecture, and was brought to northern India in the sixteenth century by its Moghol conquerors. A similar, although flatter, variant was used at the same period... in Tudor England. Here, instead of a segment of an arch in the central part, the more abrupt curves at each side are prolonged by straight lines or barely perceptible curves, which join at the central axis (between the jambs) to form the summit of the arch. In India, decorative effect is sometimes given by curving these straight lines upward just before they meet, to form a pronounced point. This effect was also used in the gothic flamboyant style of the fifteenth and sixteenth centuries. Here, the straight part was usually reduced, or even eliminated, and the two inverse curves juxtaposed.

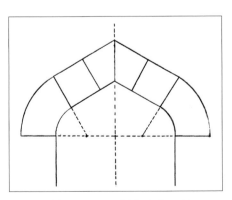

Figure 139. Persian and Moghol architecture. Often, this arch is stilted, i.e. raised by prolonging the line of the jambs before beginning the curve of the arch.

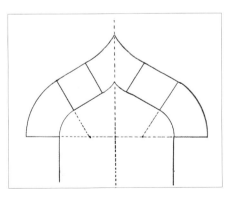

Figure 140. The same as accolade.

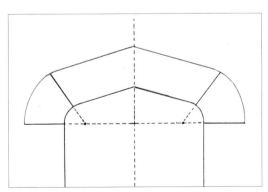

Figure 141. In Tudor architecture, the springing (beginning) of the arch is a more abrupt curve of small diameter, and the summit is lower than in the preceding examples.

Another often-used form for constructing low-summit arches is the **segmental** arch. This is a single curve, taken from a portion (**segment**) of a semicircle. In this arch, unlike the semicircular or the basket handle, there are no lateral curves to smooth out the junction of the principal curve with the jambs.

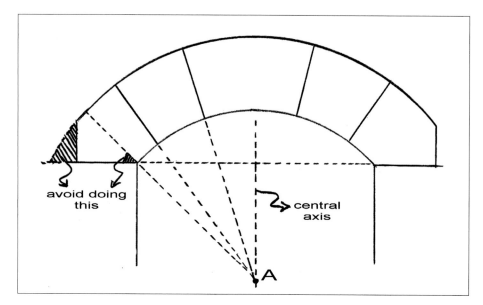

Figure 143. Any curve can be chosen ; if the center is placed higher on the mid-line, the curve will be more pronounced; if it is placed lower, the curve becomes flatter. Flattened to the extreme, it becomes a straight line (called a flat arch). But the flatter he curve, the greater are the risks of one of the stones slipping.

If the portion marked 1 of the springing stone is eliminated (AT RIGHT in the drawing above), it is easier to fit the adjoining wall stones against it, and it becomes unnecessary to cut them at an acute angle. Also, it is best to avoid making a joint passing through the point where the arch meets the jamb (as is the case with the line X), as this kind of cut makes the stone likely to slip, and also, the acute angle at 2 is difficult to cut. Nonetheless, such cases are sometimes seen.

The segmental arch was often used in the Middle Ages when setting a rabbet into a doorway. Even though the arch opening onto the facade may be semicircular or pointed, a segmental arch will be set behind this to create the rabbet while also providing an enlarged doorway on the inside, enabling the door to open inwards without butting against the sides.

Figure 144. Château de Quéribus, Aude, France; segmental arch in the foreground.

Figure 145. Spesbourg Castle, Alsace.

92

Figure 146. Bienne, Switzerland; the Ring, sixteenth century square.

In the 18th century, segmental arches were in style, both in the towns and in aristocratic country houses. Manors and castles of this period, as well as administrative buildings and houses of the wealthy were built with facades featuring the repetition of segmental-arched windows. Often their keystones were sculpted with **mascarons** (faces) or other exuberant motifs. (See also "Architectural Styles throughout the Centuries", figures 238, 241, 247 and 248).

Figures 147-148. Aix-en-Provence; 18th century.

93

One other form, sometimes found in Europe (particularly in Spain) but most common in North Africa, is the horseshoe arch. This is usually a semi-circular (but may also be a pointed) arch in which the curve is prolonged beyond (i.e. below) the horizontal line on which its center is situated; the arch thus begins to close again as it goes beyond the semicircle. This horseshoe shape was most used in Maghrebin Islamic architecture, but was also found in the kingdom established earlier by the Visigoths in Spain, from the sixth century until 711. The Visigoth arches were designed with their joints radiating from the center on their upper semi-circle, whereas below this, the stones are cut with horizontal joints to sit more stably on the jambs. In Ibiric Islamic and in North African architecture, though, the stones were often cut with their joints radiating, even below the center (see facing page). Although this system is structurally less stable, it was nonetheless favored by certain architects and/or clients from an esthetic point of view, and the stones cut in this way were often of different colors, set in alternance.

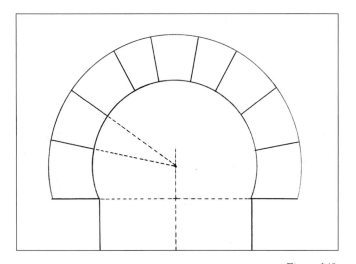

Figure 149.

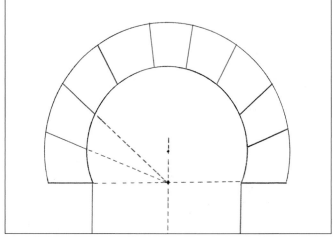

Figure 149a.

Figure 150. Visigoth church built in 661; San Juan de Baños, Castile and Leon, Spain.

Figure 151. Toledo, Spain.

Figures 152-154. Mozarabe church (constructed by Moorish artisans remaining in Christian territory after the Reconquest of their province by the kingdom of Leon); San Miguel de la Escalera, Castille and Leon, Spain.

On the FACING PAGE, horseshoe forms are seen in both foreground and background; but as these are cut into a single stone, and are not a series of assembled stones, they are not arches, but rather, lintels.

Figure 155. Tarragona, Spain.

In addition to all the foregoing well-defined and recognized categories, it must be said that an arch can be made almost any way as long as it holds up. So although the forms explained above have been tried and proven, it sometimes happens that a builder deforms or reforms one of these, either by lack of technical expertise, or deliberately, to better suit his tastes or needs. So it is with the ***rampant arches*** seen above, used in whatever form is necessary in order to compensate a difference in level; so, likewise, can we find arches such as those in figures 157 and 158.

NOTES for this chapter

*Theoretically, the arch's components are cut as wedges, that is, wider at the top than at the bottom. But in practice, arches – and vaults – are often made up of **parallelepiped** elements (i.e, with each pair of opposite sides parallel), and are not wedge-shaped. This is particularly the case with brick construction, which saw the earliest arches in Mesopotamia 5000 years ago, and this technique has endured; many examples can be seen in the brick architecture of the Mediterranean countries, from Roman times through to the present day.

To make a curve with parallelepiped elements, these must be spaced more widely at the curve's extrados. This can be done by making the mortar joint increasingly thicker from intrados to extrados; but even better, the mason can also insert some incompressible, preferably wedge-shaped, material – such as pieces of tiles or slate – into the triangular space thus formed.

The same technique can be applied to parallelepiped or to irregular stones when these are not too heavy. The fitting is obviously less precise and thus its resistance to stress will be less than maximal; but nonetheless, many such arches and vaults have survived for centuries. See also Figure 169 (title page of subchapter *Barrel Vaults*).

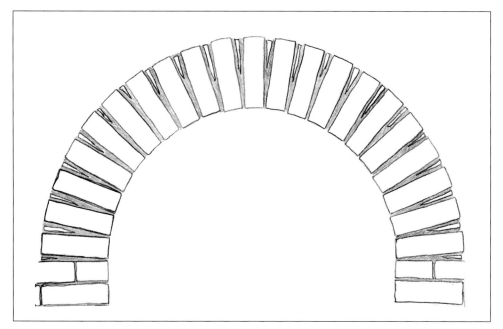

Figure 156.

Figure 157. As in the above drawing, this arch made of stones that are not cut to a wedge shape has been set up by adjusting and filling the joints with mortar and stone shims.

Figure 158. Whereas this one has been curved by using an exaggeratedly wedge-shaped keystone. Alps of Provence, France.

Figure 159. Chillon Castle, Switzerland.

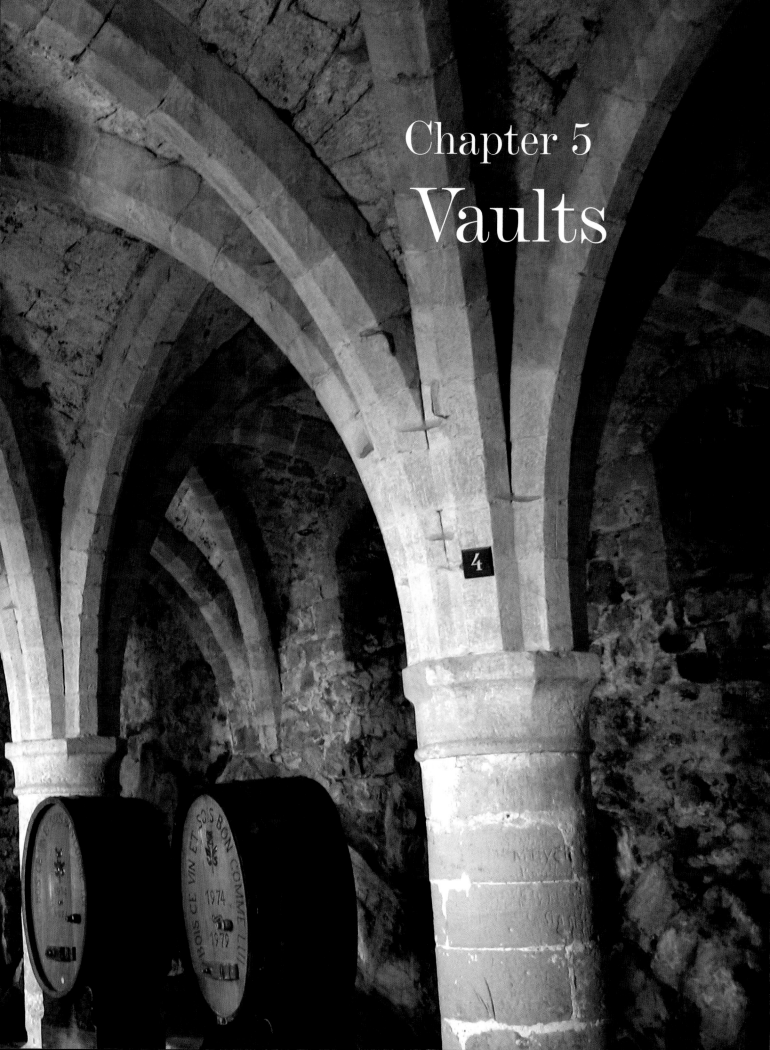

Chapter 5
Vaults

Vaults

Vaults are one possible way of covering a space enclosed by walls. But just as the function of an arch can be filled instead by a much simpler wooden lintel, so can the function of a vault be filled instead by a much more easily constructed wooden roofing system. Nonetheless, builders often preferred the stone vault. This would of course be used where wood was locally unavailable, but even where the wooden option was possible, the stone vault was often favored. In spite of its requiring much more time to build, it was more resistant and longer-lasting. Also, concerning ecclesiastic architecture, there is much support for the idea that medieval church builders considered their works not merely as meeting halls, but rather as places of spiritual transformation aided by the energy of the site. The church was consciously and conscientiously situated at a place of high telluric energy, which the vault, both by its mineral character and by its rounded form, amplified.

All of the forms used for arches, as described in the preceding chapter, can be used for vaults as well. And, as with arches, the form of the vault was often associated with particular periods and architectural styles.

The First Vaults and Domes

Archeological discoveries have revealed that vaults and domes were made of sun dried bricks both in Babylon and in Egypt, as early as 3500 BC. These vaults were probably built by leaning their constituent arches of bricks against the end wall of the room to be covered.

Their weight thus partly supported by the end wall, the bricks could be set up with a thick and sticky mud and clay mortar, which would be sufficiently adhesive to hold them in place while the arch was completed. The arches being self-supporting, the vault could then be set up one row at a time without needing to rest on a wooden frame, which was an important advantage in these countries where wood was scarce. This technique was not suitable for use with stone, however, stones being both heavier and less able to adhere to the mud mortar than are earthen bricks; it is useful, nonetheless, to situate its use in the history of architecture.

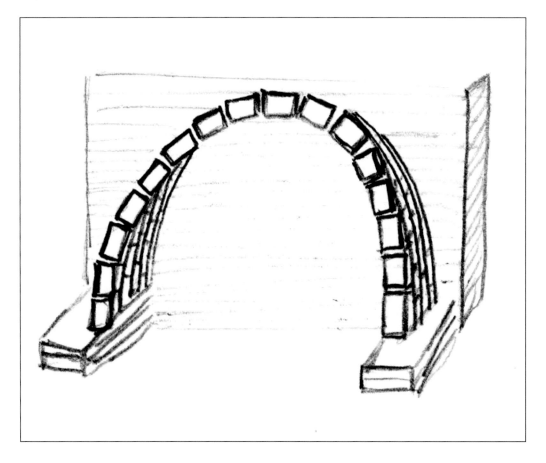

Figure 160.

Figure 161. This cross-sectional view of a ruined borie shows the horizontal set given the stones, as well as their progressive overhang from one course to another.

Corbelled Vaults

Another primitive way of setting up a vault, which was also used with circular constructions to make domes, is ***corbelling***. This technique uses stones set horizontally, with each course slightly overhanging the one preceding it. The overhang must be slight enough that the piled-up stones do not collapse as more weight is added to the pile. The summit, where the two sides meet, is covered over by a course of wide, flat, stones. If the stones making up the two walls have been set tilted slightly outward, no other roofing material is needed. Round and elliptical huts were also constructed; roofed over with corbelled domes, and this form is even more stable than the rectangle.

Figures 161-165. All photos in these figures show bories from Upper Provence.

103

Figures 166-167. Corbelled domes on circular bories in Upper Provence.

Corbelled vaults and domes were in use as early as the Mycenaean period of ancient Greece, as can be seen in the "tomb of Atrius", with a domed circular chamber of 12 m in diameter, built around 1325 BC. From that time onwards, and until fairly recently (18th century, for the *bories* of Haute Provence), this technique has been used all around the northern shore of the Mediterranean Sea in simple, generally pastoral, constructions. A completely different civilization and architecture also used it, in Asia, for the building of the Khmer temple complexes (Angkor Wat and its many neighbors, Cambodia). These temples, built toward the end of the 12th century, are characterized by a series of rooms connected by long, narrow, passageways, these being covered over by large slabs of corbelled cut stone.

Figure 168. Village des Bories, Gordes, Provence.

Barrel Vaults

The barrel vault is like an arch extended through a certain depth, in the manner of a tunnel. It can take any of the forms shown in the chapter *ARCHES*; semicircular, pointed, basket handle, or any other; these are simply prolonged to make the vault.

Figure 169. This vaulted passageway, in the old town of Eze (Alpes Maritimes, France), is one of many examples of the use of irregular fieldstone for building vaults. The stones are set up on a wooden form (here, semicircular); a lime mortar sufficiently liquid to seep through the spaces between the stones is then poured from above. The mortar must harden before the form is taken down; the crust of mortar on the intrados bears the imprint of the boards. See also the note at the end of Chapter 4, p 99, about setting up arches with irregular stones.

The barrel vault, where stones cut with radiating joints were set up on temporary forms in the same way as were arches, was much used by the Romans, particularly in its semicircular form. Its principal function was to cover tunnel-like passageways in the thick walls of large public buildings such as arenas and theatres. But triumphal arches, aqueducts, and bridges, can also be considered to be barrel vaults, because of their considerable thickness (depth).

It was customary to cover temples and basilicas with wooden roofing structures, but the roman builders nonetheless used vaulting to cover certain public buildings, such as the baths of Caracalla and the basilica of Constantine, and spanned the Pantheon with a dome.*

Figures 170-171. Arena of Arles, in Provence (Provincia Romana); built at the end of the first century AD,

Figure 172. The Roman aqueduct of Segovia, Spain; end of the first century AD.

After the fall of the Western Roman Empire, the ensuing disorder resulted in the general neglect of building, and in the falling out of use of classical building skills and techniques, for a period of at least 500 years in western and central Europe.** At certain rather rare periods, these techniques reappeared for a time, in, for instance, the churches of the Visigoth kingdom established in Spain***, and in several churches and palaces built under the reign of Charlemagne and his immediate successors****.

But the greatest and longest lasting resurgence of classical building techniques occurred following the year 1000, encouraged by a long period of (relative) peace, and by the ascendancy, in almost all the kingdoms and principalities of western and central Europe, of the Roman Catholic Church. During this period of relative stability, the church had the power to tax the entire population, as well as to solicit important donations, in land or in money, from the nobility. They were thus able to obtain property and pay for the building of more, and often, of more sumptuous, churches and monasteries than at any time previously. But as building skills and techniques had fallen into disuse during the preceding centuries – after a long period of restrained activity, the builders had to practically rediscover the crafts. Their most important source of knowledge and of inspiration lay in the classical buildings which had been reused, or had fallen into ruin, and were still to be found abundantly from Asia Minor to England to North Africa.

Little by little, and over several generations, the builders taught themselves to reproduce – sometimes imperfectly – what they were thus able to observe. The result was the flowering of that art called Romanesque, which visibly has its roots in classical Roman (and through it, Greek) construction, but with the spirit of a new and greatly transformed society. This art form gave in turn, after flourishing for a century and a half, the basis of knowledge and techniques necessary for the development of "Gothic" art, which then progressively succeeded it. The mutation of the one into the other was especially a result of developments in vaulting techniques, as we shall see.

Figure 173. Capitals with sculpted acanthus leaves; cloister of the cathedral of Vaison la Romaine, Provence.

Figures 174-175. Triangular fronton, columns topped with capitals sculpted with acanthus leaves, archivolts decorated with darts and oves are some of the elements directly copied from classical architecture. But the naive sculptures on the tympanum and on the fronton show a different spirit, characteristic (among other things) of Romanesque art. Saint Gabriel's chapel, near the old Roman city of Arles, Provence.

The structural characteristic of barrel vaults is the force they exert on the walls, pushing them outward. The walls must consequently be thick enough to resist this force. A modern engineer could certainly calculate all the forces at work, but medieval builders determined wall thickness intuitively and by experience. The walls of small churches chapels are usually about 80 cm thick; those of the bigger ones are double that thickness. The window openings in the sidewalls are necessarily small to avoid weakening the structure. Sometimes it was necessary, either in anticipation of the lateral forces or to correct an unfortunate lack of anticipation, to incorporate – or to add on – buttresses.

Figure 176. Buttresses in a Romanesque church; Zamora, Spain.

On its inside, the barrel vault was often reinforced by one or more ***doubleaux***, or ***traverse ribs***, arches which span the nave, dividing it into sections. This, although not a necessity, nonetheless contributes to the strength of the structure (and also allows for the construction of the nave one section at a time, with the supporting framework being moved and reused each time a section is added).

When this system of skeletal support is used, the buttresses are placed against the walls at points corresponding to the positions of the pillars supporting the *doubleaux*.

Cross Vaults

In the cross vault, two barrel vaults interpenetrate at right angles, or almost. Their intersections are marked by well-defined edges, as can be seen in the photos below.

Figure 177. Interpenetration of two barrel vaults to form a cross vault; Romanesque cloister of the cathedral of Vaison-la -Romaine, Provence.

Figure 178. Cross vaults with ribs; Chateau de Queribus, Aude, France.

Whereas the thrusts of a barrel vault occur along its entire length, those of a cross vault are concentrated only at the four corners from which it springs. The space between these points can consequently be opened up as long as these points are shored up by equivalent resisting forces.

The cross vault was not an innovation of the Gothic builders; it was already a feature of many Romanesque churches, be it to open passageways between the nave and the parallel aisles, or in the cloisters, to allow the surrounding walkways to interpenetrate at their meeting points. The builders were surely conscious that they could use such vaults to also open the naves to the light of the sky, if only they could find a way to ensure the stability of such huge vaults raised so high.

Figure 179. Cross vault; Dubrovnik, Croatia.

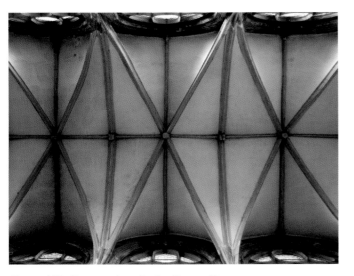

Figure 180. Cross vault with ribs; Rouen, France.

Figure 181. Flying buttresses crowned with pinnacles; Rodez Cathedral, France.

One of the innovations in this direction derived from the practice, noted earlier, of using **traverse arches** as a supporting framework for the barrel vaults covering naves and aisles. This idea was applied to the cross vault, and resulted in a framework of crossing diagonal **ribs** independent of the mass, which could support an infill of stones wedging against one another. The separation of the ribs from the mass allowed for the use of thinner, lighter stones as infill, and also allowed a greater flexibility of the whole, as the infill could move somewhat on its framework without breaking in case of settling. Also, with the use of ribs, the architect could more precisely direct the thrusts of the vault, and thus counteract them more efficiently. A system of counter-thrusts had, of course, to be devised, and these often took the graceful form of **flying buttresses**, arches springing from fixed buttresses set all along the nave and around the apse opposite each of the pillars supporting the vault. These arches curve inward to support the walls very high up, at points just above the springing points of the ribs, precisely at those places where the outward thrusts are the strongest. They lean in on an angle with a very important horizontal component, increasing the efficiency of the counter-thrust. Buttresses and flying buttresses are crowned with *pinnacles* of stone rising to a point, their edges sculpted with stylized leaves. The pinnacles serve not only as decoration, but also add weight to the buttresses, thus increasing their stability.

The use of the pointed arch was another determining factor in the development of Gothic architecture, for the crossing of two semicircular barrel vaults would not have given a satisfactory result, as their limited heights do not give the visual impression of reaching toward the sky. Their diagonal arches (the *ogives*, forming the ribs) would also have been too flat, for rotating an arch through 30 or 45 ° while making it span the same distance between two parallel walls makes a much flatter arch, whose thrusts have a more important horizontal component, augmenting the forces tending to topple the supporting pillars. You can judge this for yourself by referring to Figure 183.

The pointed arch was sometimes used in Romanesque churches, but it was only when the builders combined this with the cross vault that the latter's possibilities were increased. The different possible forms of pointed arches (see Ch 4) enable the builder to adjust the height of any given arch at will, and thus allow the crossing of vaults of different widths, as their summits can be adjusted to reach a common height. This is impossible with the semicircular arch, whose height depends on its diameter.*****

The semicircular arch is nonetheless very important in gothic architecture. This is because the ***ogives*** (diagonal ribs) are usually determined as semicircles, and the side and end arches of the crossing vaults are subsequently given that pointed form which enables their summits to cross at a common level.

The new style evolved incessantly over two centuries, leading to many modifications of the decorative details: the pillars were given moldings emphasizing their verticality; capitals and *abaci* were reduced in volume and finally eliminated altogether; the effect was a very ethereal architecture – a prowess, considering the enormous mass of stone involved. While we can say that the small Romanesque church seems attached to the Earth and has a cave-like atmosphere, the Gothic cathedral gives the impression of reaching for the sky, with its tall pillars and its high, pointed vaults.

Figure 183. Gallery of the Romanesque cloister of St. Bertrand de Comminges, in the French Pyrenées: We can see here how the sections of the gallery, each one under its cross vault, open onto both the cloister (at right) and along the gallery passageway. The utility of such an opening for a new, more airy architecture can be imagined; nonetheless, it can be seen here that the crossing of these two rather low-summit arches, one semicircular and the other segmental, produces **ogives** *(diagonal arches) which are consequently very low, and are incompatible with the spirit of such an architecture (the Gothic), which requires the crossing of higher, more elegant pointed arches.*

NOTES for this chapter

*These buildings were constructed at Rome itself, where architecture was liberated from its usual constraints by the use of Roman cement. This was made by using pozzolan, from crushed volcanic stone found in deposits nearby, as an aggregate in place of sand. This concrete, into which also went a good quantity of gravel and small stones, hardened with lime to form a very solid mass. When such a mass – in the form of a vault or a dome, in the cases we are considering – is set atop load-bearing walls, it exerts its weight exclusively downward, without any sideways component. Without lateral thrusts, the walls can carry heavier loads; domes and vaults can thus be much more vast. In Imperial Rome, several enormous vaults and domes were built to cover certain thermal baths (those of Diocletian and of Caracalla), as well as the basilica of Constantine. The latter used not only barrel vaults, but also had a vast central hall covered with a cross vault. But because of the specific nature of the pozzolan and its limited geographic zone of availability, these techniques were used only in Rome itself, and did not really mark the architecture of the provinces.

In the East, on the other hand, Byzantium remained powerful, and even took in many artisans fleeing Rome. The Eastern Empire had its own distinctive traditions because of its constant interaction (often warlike) with its powerful Persian neighbor, and went in a different architectural direction. Here, the basilica, inspiration and model for the churches of the young but very dynamic Church of Rome (Roman Catholic), was left aside, and the churches of the East were mainly built in the form of a Greek cross (all four branches of equal length), and covered in their center by a dome. The architects of Justinian (emperor from 527 until 565) and his successors elaborated a system for setting the round base of a dome onto a square-shaped support by the use of **trompes (*squinch arches*) in the angles (see Figure 208). The principle of passing from a square to a circle through an octagon, using arches to obliquely span the corners, or filling them with sloping *pendentives* (see Figure 209), had already been practiced, but the *trompe* was more elegant and the transition more graceful.

The forms and methods developed by Byzantium became the heritage of all those countries which adopted the Eastern Church (Orthodox), and were used to build the medieval churches of Greece, Serbia, and Bulgaria, and later, Russia and Ukraine. Armenia, midway between the Byzantine and the Persian Empires, inherited from both of these influences, and often acted as a transmitter.

***These former barbarians, ravagers of Rome (in 410), settled in Spain later in the same century, where their customs and practices evolved to exhibit an increasing gentility. Like other former barbarian tribes who became masters of territories abandoned by Rome (Ostrogoths and Lombards in Italy, Franks and Burgundians in France, Angles and Saxons in Britain), they adopted Christianity. Several of the churches that their kings ordered constructed during the 7th and early 8th centuries are still intact. Among them are: San Juan de Baños, San Pedro de la Nave, Santa Maria de Melque, and Santa Maria de Lara.

****Among others: the Palatine Chapel at Aix-la-Chapelle (Aachen, 792 to 805), and the gatehouse of the monastery of Lorsch (800).

*****Earlier Romanesque builders experimenting with the concept of crossing semicircular barrel vaults of unequal diameters tried to resolve the problem by stilting the smaller of the two – that is, by raising its springing point above that of the bigger arch – but the result always appears clumsy.

Chapter 6
Architecture through the Centuries

Figure 184. This very simple building is made entirely of unshaped fieldstone, and has a roof with a single slope. It is probably from the nineteenth century, and served as a storage shed for workers in the vineyards, but in a way, it is completely timeless, in that it is not the product of a style or technique that identifies it as belonging to a certain age.

The choir of a Romanesque church is usually made up of one or several rounded *apses*, although in some cases, it can be a simple rectangle. Apses are lower than the nave, and are covered with a half dome, which is then built up with rubble masonry to create a cone-shaped roof that will shed the rainwater.

In the two cases shown here, the apses are marked with *Lombardian bands*, a sort of frieze of arches in relief which can be seen at the tops of the apse walls. These are named after their conceptors, or at least, their propagators – teams of itinerant masons originally from the north of Italy. Their services were much in demand, and they often traveled far afield.

Figure 185. Romanesque church in the countryside just inland from Ventimiglia, Italy, eleventh century.

Figure 186. Church of the Abbey of St. Martin du Canigou, Pyrenées Orientales, France, eleventh century.

Figure 187. Interior of the Visigoth church of San Pedro de la Nave, Spain, with its horseshoe arches. Built at the end of the seventh century.

The choir of a church, seen here at the back of the photo, is the part where the altar is usually found – usually in or just immediately in front of the main apse – and where the priest performs the ceremonies. It is the focal point of the church, both for the attention of the assembly, as well as from an energetic point of view. It is almost always oriented in an easterly direction (to within about 20°). Some think that this is in homage to Jerusalem; others, to the rising sun. One theory states that, like Stonehenge and several other megalithic sites, the orientation of medieval churches was established on an axis determined by a first stake driven into the ground at a place chosen for the quality of its telluric energy, and completed by the positioning of another stake aligned with the first one and the rising sun at the moment when it appears on the horizon. But whereas the orientation of megalithic sites was established at winter or summer solstices, or at some other astrological event of importance to their builders, the orientation of a medieval church was determined by the alignment with the rising sun on the day of the saint to whom the church was dedicated. Some questions remain unsolved by current theories, though; I have often observed, for instance, that the nave is not necessarily in exactly the same alignment as the apse.

Figure 188. Entranceway to the Romanesque church of Villefranche de Conflent, Pyrenées Orientales, France, made entirely of local marble.

Figure 189. A capital from the same church.

Figure 190. Cloister of the monastery San Benet de Bages, in Catalonia, Spain, beginning of the twelfth century. Cloisters are a part of almost every medieval monastery or abbey, as well as of many cathedrals. Their function is to provide a place of tranquility for rest and meditation, especially for meditation in movement, for the monks or nuns could walk in the peripheral passages of this quadrangle without leaving the shelter of the monastery walls.

This cloister is typically Romanesque by its double columns topped with sculpted capitals supporting semicircular arcades which open onto the central garden. It is atypical by the proportions of its openings, the columns being shorter and the arches wider than those usually found in Romanesque cloisters.

Figure 191. Just 40 km distant lies the monastery of Lluça. Here, as in all Romanesque cloisters, we find a series of semicircular arches set atop columns and capitals. But unlike those habitually seen in other cloisters, here the columns are single instead of paired. End of the twelfth century.

Figures 192-193. Ávila, Spain.

The **twinned (or geminée) window,** with its two openings separated by a colonette with a capital (there also exists a triple version), is often used in medieval architecture, be it ecclesiastic, civil, or castral. In the twelfth and thirteenth centuries, it is usually made with semicircular arches, but pointed arches appear progressively during this period, and supersede them in the fourteenth. When the openings are small and the stones available as lintels are large, the two openings can be cut into the monolithic lintel. But most often, arches, composed of three or more stones, are constructed. Although this requires more time, it is much more reliable, as the monolithic lintels are apt to break under stress, as has visibly occurred in Figure 193.

Figure 195. Cahors, France.

Figure 194. Visigoth church San Pedro de la Nave, province of Zamora, Spain.

118

Figure 196. Château de Chillon, Switzerland.

Windows became increasingly sophisticated in the following centuries. Those with pointed arches, elaborated when the Gothic style passed into civil architecture, often display very complex moldings, and are sometimes made with trefoils and/or with an archivolt (Figure 197). See also figures 211 to 214, for a variant much used in Venice and its dependent cities on the Dalmatian coast. Although this style generally went into disuse at the Renaissance, those windows that still display it at that time become heavy with decoration, especially in Spain (Figure 198).

Figure 197. Sarlat, Dordogne, France.

Figure 198. Zamora, Spain.

119

Figure 199. Tarragona, Spain.

Oculi are sometimes used in the facades of Romanesque churches, or in some early Gothic churches (like that Figure 201) where the builders were too timid to open the walls further.

Figure 200. Girona, Spain.

Figure 201. Korčula, Dalmatia, Croatia.

Figures 202-203. Cathedral of Rouen, France.

How is it possible to realize a work as fine, as airy, as fragile, and yet as enormous as a Gothic rose window? The answer is simple, although its execution is not: by dividing it into many pieces. The rose is in fact an assemblage of stones whose forms and dimensions have been carefully calculated by the master stonecutter. He must divide the ensemble so that each piece can be cut from a manipulable block, yet does not become extremely fragile, while remaining as simple as possible in its technical realization. When the stones are assembled, the joints will hardly be noticeable, being so small in relation to the whole. And, in view of the height of the rose, the observer on the ground is too far away to distinguish them. But if a detail of the accompanying photo is enlarged and the line of the joints accentuated, you can see how the stones have been assembled.

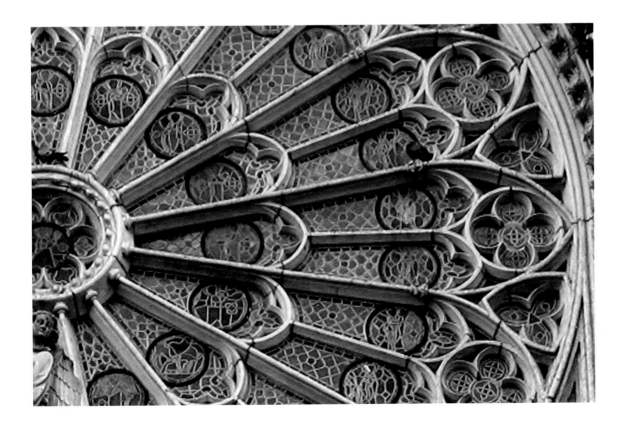

Figure 204.

Medieval towns and villages were usually surrounded by protecting walls. If the village was under the protection of a castle, which was often the case (at least in theory), the castle could also be enclosed within the village walls, which would serve as its first line of defense. Certain villages (here, Lacoste, in Provence) still retain greater or lesser portions of their former defensive walls. Several fortified openings allowed for controlled access to the town. These gateways could be very effectively barricaded in case of attack. Note the thickness of the wall, with a second doorframe inside the first. Against the second was set a metallic grid, called a ***portcullis,*** normally raised. When lowered into place, this would block the opening. In front of the portcullis, a substantial wooden door of two equal sections, opening in the middle, was set on large swivel pins fixed securely in the masonry. The door was at least two boards thick, and nailed together with iron nails whose sizeable heads further protected the wood. Its opening was blocked from the inside by a large wooden beam, which was slid into a hole left for this purpose in the masonry on either side of the doorway, and prevented its being pushed inwards.

Note also the ***machicolation*** of cut stone protruding over the gateway. Through these, the defenders could drop boulders or anything else at hand on their attackers, while a hail of arrows from the wall added to the latter's difficulties. A walkway ran along the inside of the ramparts near their summit to allow the defenders easy access to all parts of the wall, to parry attacks wherever they might occur. (See FACING PAGE, BOTTOM.)

Figure 205.

The village of Oppède, built on a hill rising from the foot of the Luberon mountain in Provence, clearly shows the typical form of medieval villages, even though it has completely fallen into ruin in its central parts. At the summit is the castle, surrounded by ramparts, just below this, the church, and further below, the village. The houses that remain are mostly those of the important families of the seventeenth and eighteenth centuries, which had already replaced, at their time, the houses of the peasants and artisans in the village's lower parts.

Figure 206. The walkway giving access to the top of the town's fortifications; Murten, Switzerland.

123

Figure 207.

The **trompe** permits the builder to pass from a square base to a round dome. Much used in Byzantine, and then in Greek architecture for this purpose, it also allows any fantasy where something protruding above a receding angle would not normally find sufficient support. In the case of this bridge over the Aigue Brune, in Provence, the road must turn sharply to cross the river.

As can be seen, the trompe is closely related to the arc, but with an extra dimension, forming a cone around its center point.

Figure 208. Cupola poised on pendentives (Dordogne, France).

Figure 209. Cupola poised on trompes, Arles, Provence, France.

125

Figures 210-212.

The Republic of Ragusa (now the city of Dubrovnik, in Croatia), even though independent of the Republic of Venice since 1350, was nonetheless greatly influenced by the latter in its architecture. This influence can be seen in the building at the end of the street, a palace from the first half of the sixteenth century. Quarries of hard limestone on the nearby island of Korčula provided the stone for these buildings.

Other cities on the Dalmatian coast, such as Hvar, Split, and Trogir, which remained under the sway of Venice until 1797 (date at which Napoleon put an end to its existence as a republic), also show Venetian characteristics. In the accompanying photos, we see Venetian varieties of Gothic flamboyant windows, with trefoils and often with archivolts in the form of an accolade.

126

Figures 213-214.

Venetian architecture, heavily influenced by the Gothic Flamboyant, sometimes uses **overlapping arches** in its palaces. As can be seen at the upper story of the two buildings shown here, overlapping two semicircular arches produces three pointed arches. At the lower story of the building ABOVE, we can see that overlapping two pointed arches produces three lancet arches. Hvar, Dalmatia, Croatia.

Figure 214a.

Mullioned windows appear at the time of the Renaissance (which in Italy covered the fifteenth and sixteenth centuries; in France, a few decades later). They are part of a general improvement in the conditions of comfort that characterized that period – at least, for the wealthy. Their intention was to increase the dimensions of the windows. But as the glass-making techniques of the time only allowed the making of small panes, the space between the framing elements could not be too great. Hence, the very large window opening was subdivided by the insertion of ***mullions***, vertical and horizontal framing elements of cut stone. These were usually cut with a molding, which could be as simple as a chamfer, or become quite complex, depending on the fortune of the owner. During the following centuries, the possibility of making larger panels of glass allowed for fairly large windows without the incorporation of mullions. Moreover, the systems of taxation at the time often calculated residential worth by the number of windows, and mullioned windows counted as four. Consequently, many homeowners in succeeding generations walled up three of the four openings, or tore out the mullions. Such modifications can often be read on the facades of surviving buildings.

Figures 215-217.

Inner courtyard of the royal castle of Pau, in the French Pyrénées. Its facades are typical of the Renaissance, displaying mullioned windows of differing degrees of complexity, reflecting the status of the person living in, or the guests lodged in, the room in question. The main doors display basket-handle arches, and these too have moldings of varying degrees of complexity.

This mullioned window (Figure 218) displays only the most simple decoration, a chamfer around each of the four openings. This is nonetheless enough to greatly refine the otherwise graceless mullions.

The window below (Figure 219) shows a very complex molding, often seen, in one or another of its variations, at the time. The most important protruding element is called a ***tore,*** which is often accompanied, as here, by a ***listel.*** Tores and listels can be repeated on the inside – or, more rarely, on the outside – of the frame. The cross-section (which, when drawn on a piece of stiff material, serves as the template for marking the stones to be cut to the same model) is shown on the opposite page.

Figure 218. Beynac, Dordogne.

Figure 219. Vaison la Romaine, Provence.

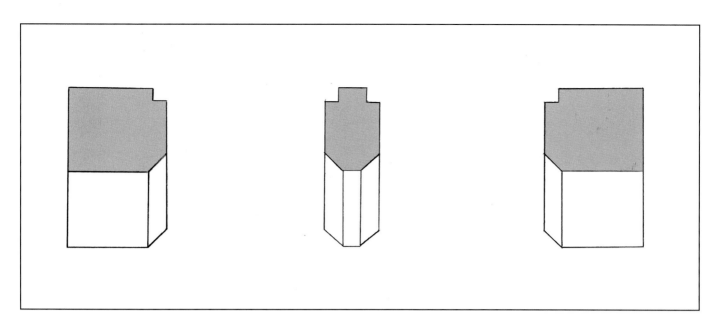

The accompanying drawing shows a cross-section through the jambs. The dotted line indicates the initial volume of the block before cutting; the grey surface represents the cross-section as viewed from above, which is also the template to be used for cutting the stones. Note that the listel is in the same plane as the front surface of the block, which simplifies somewhat the execution of the piece. (See the technical chapter on *MOLDINGS*, in *THE STONEWORKERS' HANDBOOK*, for further explanation.)

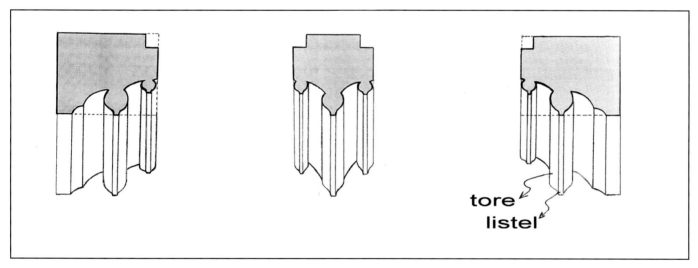

Figures 220-221.

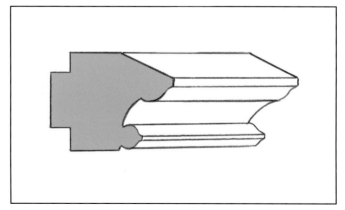

Figure 222.

The moldings run along the two jambs and the vertical mullion, as well as along the underside of the lintels and of the horizontal mullions. The upper sides of the horizontal mullions, shown in the above drawing, are cut with a slope to shed the rainwater. Note, in Figure 219, how all the elements of the molding penetrate one another at their horizontal and vertical junction points.

131

Figures 224-225. Vaison la Romaine, Provence.

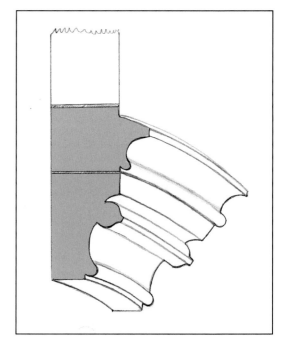

Figure 223.

Doorways with basket-handle arches, common during the Renaissance, can also show complex moldings, including even tores and listels, Note how the molding of the arch *expires* into that of the jambs.

Figure 226. Ansouis, Provence.

The Renaissance, a period of greater stability and security than the preceding two centuries, witnessed the demilitarization of castles and of the homes of the wealthy. Often, in the civil architecture of the time, angle turrets are added, although these no longer have any military function. Placed on the façade, these structures become window bays called oriels. At the beginning of the Renaissance period, when the Gothic style was becoming common in civil architecture, they are often decorated, as seen here, with friezes of arcs with trefoils.

Figure 227. Nuremberg, Germany.

Figure 228. Zug, Switzerland.

Figures 229-230. Oriels in the Engadina Valley, canton Graubunden, Switzerland.

In Alpine countries, where the rough stone masonry is most often lime-plastered, the form of the oriel is sufficient to make it stand out on the façade as a decorative element. In the second half of the sixteenth century, though, the domination of the baroque style produced a flourish of details in the sculpted decoration, as well as in the painted décor which was characteristic of the Alpine regions, and especially, of the Austrian Tirol.

Figure 231. Colmar, Alsace, France

Figure 232. Canton Graubunden, Switzerland.

Figure 233. West Tirol, Austria.

Figures 234-235.

At this same period, the facades become a support for panels of extravagant decoration, often displaying very intricate carving. In Spain, the **"*plateresque*"** ("silversmith") style was in vogue in the first half of the sixteenth century, and produced works such as the facades of the University of Salamanca and of the School of the Minor Friars, on the same square, both of which are shown in the accompanying photos.

The Casa de las Conchas (the House of the Shells, opposite page), built at the same period, does not display the same flourish of intricate carving, but the methodical spacing and repetition of the sculpted shells creating an effect of ***clair-obscure*** (light and shadow) reveals the same desire to decorate the facades.

The plateresque style characterized Spanish architecture of the period; as this was transposed to the New World, it profoundly marked the architecture of Latin America, and particularly Mexico, for a century more.

Figures 236-237.

Decor of scallop-shells on the sunny façade of the Casa de las Conchas, Salamanca, Spain. The shells are the commonly recognized symbol of the pilgrimage to Santiago de Compostello (St. James), whose major route passed not far to the north. Although it is possible to sculpt the shells directly into the mass of a stone block, this becomes difficult when they overlap two (or more) stones; even then, it is possible by splitting up the sculpture into perfectly fitted parts, but this has not been done here, otherwise, a joint would be visible. Instead, the masons have fixed the shells, sculpted separately, onto the wall.

Figure 238. Basel, Switzerland.

Figure 239. Church of St. Nikolai, St Petersburg, Russia.

Figures 240-241. Aix-en-Provence, France.

In the seventeenth century, the more imposing architecture took a more classical direction (that is, of ancient Greco-Roman inspiration). Monumental doorways are often seen surrounded by a series of moldings, pillars in low relief on either side of the door, and complex **entablatures** (protruding bands of moldings above and parallel to the lintel or arch), sometimes supporting balconies. The moldings, complex though they are, were nonetheless a simplification in comparison to the Renaissance, in that in spite of the multitude of changes in level, which light and shadow turn into visible lines, these are fairly shallow; elements such as the *tores* have disappeared. Although the sculpted décor can include wreaths and garlands, this is derived directly from classical Roman architecture, and is generally more sober than in the preceding baroque period. Even so, some of the exuberant baroque motifs may be carried on, as can be seen in figures 238 and 239. Windows are also simplified, single openings now

replacing mullioned windows. In those buildings built with an ample budget, architects designed symmetrical facades with rhythmic repetition of the windows on the upper floors; these often featured keystones sculpted with undulating leaves or **mascarons** (faces, both beautiful and grotesque) in high relief (see Figure 238, and also Figure 148 in Ch 4). Whereas in the seventeenth century doors and windows featured either straight lintels or semi-circular arches, in the eighteenth, they habitually used segmental arches with a subtle curve. Some commentators attempt to classify different periods within these two centuries according to certain characteristics, but it seems to me that there are too many variables and exceptions to be able to do this with much accuracy. Let us say simply that the similarities of style within this period are much greater than the differences, compared with the preceding and with the following centuries.

Figures 242-250. The villages of Provence contain many doorways from the seventeenth and eighteenth centuries; these are much more numerous than examples from preceding centuries, as the villages suffered much destruction during the religious wars of the sixteenth and early seventeenth centuries. The following pages contain a sampling. These are usually more modest than the architecture of Aix-en Provence (seen on the preceding page), which was the capital and most prominent city of the region at the time.

140

Figures 242-245. Seventeenth century doorways in Provence.

Figures 247-248. Eighteenth century houses in Provence.

Figures 249-250. Eighteenth century doorways in Provence.

Part Two
The Stoneworker's Handbook

Figure 250a.

Figure 251.

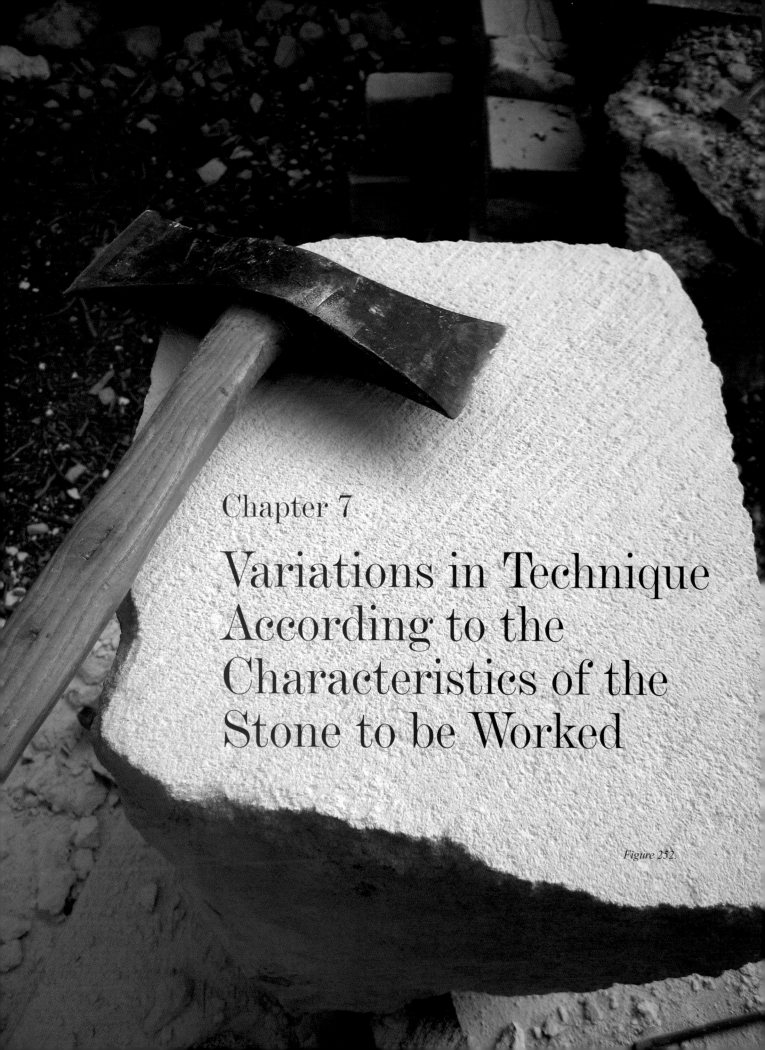

Chapter 7

Variations in Technique According to the Characteristics of the Stone to be Worked

Figure 252.

Variations in Technique According to the Characteristics of the Stone to be Worked

Although each kind of stone has its particularities, we can distinguish two major categories, each of which requires specific tools and methods somewhat different from the other. These are: **soft stones, and hard stones.**

It is, then, not really necessary for a stonecutter to have a highly developed knowledge of geology; he need not even know the geological classification of a stone to be able to work it, but must feel how it reacts to his tools. Once the apprentice is familiar with the method of shaping any one kind of stone, he can decide, after ten seconds of experimenting with an unfamiliar variety, which tools and methods should be used to work it.

Soft Stones

In this category we find most limestones (but not all; some limestones are very hard, and these will be treated in the section on hard stones). Soft limestones are found in many parts of France (Normandy, the Parisian basin, Charente, Poitou, Provence, and others), and are found throughout the world, most countries having limestone deposits somewhere within their borders. These can be of different colors, but most often they are light-colored, and even white. Alabaster (white, grey, pink, etc.) and soapstone (usually grey or green) are often used in sculpture, but rarely in building. These are so soft that they can be sculpted with a knife or a chisel held in the hand, without the use of a mallet, except for making a rough cut where much material must be removed.

Chisels cut into soft stone, whereas with hard stone, they chip off pieces.

The photo shows the basic tools for use with soft stone. The demonstration *Dressing a Face and Squaring a Stone with Precision* is done with these tools on a soft limestone from Provence. It can be applied also to hard stone, with the modifications noted below.

Figure 253. The basic stonecutting tools are simple: a stone axe (this one weighs 2.5 kg), a mallet (this one weighing 1 kg), a chisel with a straight cutting edge (this one is 25 mm wide), and a toothed chisel. Also required are a pencil, two rulers or other straight edges at least 80 cm long, and a square measuring about 30X40 cm.

Figure 254. A few other tools can be added to the basic equipment, though, as they are more efficient for certain operations; among them, the most useful are: a round (or conical) mallet (1kg), a lightweight mallet (750 gm), a pitching chisel (the red tool), and chisels of different widths. For cutting moldings, gouges (curved chisels—not shown here) are useful also (see the chapter on Moldings).

Hard Stones

In this category, we find basalt (so hard to shape that it is normally used in its natural state), gneiss (likewise), shale (which does not easily lend itself to shaping, although it is possible to dress a face if necessary), granite, marble, and other hard limestones. These latter three categories are often shaped. When hard stones are hit with a chisel, the tool sends chips flying (be careful for your eyes) – unless the chisel rebounds, in which case you should use a pointed chisel instead.

Shale and sandstone require a particular treatment, which will be explained later in this chapter.

Figure 255. The basic tools for shaping hard stone: a mallet (round or square) weighing 1.000 or 1.250 kg, a pitching chisel, and a pointed chisel.

The Differences between the Methods

(which beginners will understand better after having read – and experienced – the demonstrations *Roughly Dressing Hard Stone*, and *Dressing a Face and Squaring a Stone with Precision,* which follow).

Cutting Along a Line:

For soft stone, it is usual to use a chisel with a wooden handle; but for hard stone, an all-metal chisel is necessary. (In earlier centuries, these were forged from iron; in modern times, from steel.) The wooden handle provides a certain resilience when struck. This is helpful when shaping soft stone, but undesirable with hard stone. If you have trouble procuring wooden-handled tools, all metal tools will do, and are even obligatory for working hard stone. Used on hard stone, wooden handles will split in very little time, even when bound with a metal ring at either end, as is customary.

Making a Rough Cut:

For soft stone, I find the pointed-toothed chisel to be the most efficient tool. (There are also flat-toothed chisels, but these remove the matter in much smaller pieces.) Alternatively, this work can be done with a pointed chisel – usually by working diagonally across the surface in parallel lines – or even, if other tools are lacking, with an ordinary (flat-ended) chisel.

For hard stone, the rough cut is done almost exclusively with the pointed chisel, because the teeth of the toothed chisel are likely to break. The work may be done in parallel lines, but some stonecutters (myself among them) prefer working everywhere and anywhere on the surface, looking to see where and at what angle it is best to place the chisel point for the next blow. With a bit of practice, this can be done without breaking rhythm.

Finishing the Surface:

Chisels with a point or with a very small cutting edge bite more deeply into the stone than do wider chisels, and thus break off bigger chips. For this reason, these tools can be used to rough-cut all kinds of stones, but the surface is usually finished with wide-edged tools – wide chisels or stone axes – when dealing with soft stones. With hard stones, these tools are usually ineffective, as they are quickly blunted and make little impression; instead, pointed chisels are used for the finish as well as for the rough work. As the rough cut becomes increasingly refined, the stonecutter uses finer points, and/or strikes the chisel more lightly – perhaps even using a lighter hammer. The surface will inevitably be pockmarked, and never smooth, (unless finished by many increasingly finer passages and polished), because the stone is always broken off in chips, even though these become progressively smaller. Nonetheless, the surface must be level (plane), at least within the limits of tolerance upon which you have decided. These can be as fine as 1 mm, but some hollows due to bigger chips breaking off are inevitable. Different degrees of refinement of the finished surface are shown on the following page.

Some stonecutters do a final passage with the ***boucharde*** or ***bush-hammer***, whose head is made up of pyramid-shaped points. This does the job more rapidly; personally, though, I don't like the aspect given the surface by the uniform spacing of the points.

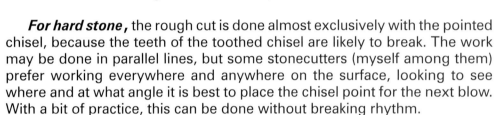

Figures 258-261. These photos show different finishes which can be obtained with the pointed chisel. The two examples in Figures 258 and 259 are fairly rough, whereas the two shown in Figures 260 and 261 are more refined, and the periphery has been Chiseled out with a flat-ended chisel. See Chapters 8 and 9.

The Particularities of Sandstone

Sandstone is made up of grains of sand cemented together by the percolation of rainwater bearing dissolved chemical elements (often silicate). It is consequently very abrasive, and quickly dulls the tools used to work it. In Alsace, in Switzerland, and in Germany, a wooden mallet with a conical head is used to strike chisels made entirely of metal. (See Figure 263.) This is undoubtedly the most efficient way of working this stone – a tradition is not maintained without reason – but a metal hammer will nonetheless do the job correctly (although the blows soon produce a ringing in the ears, and earplugs are advised).

For the rough cut, the pointed chisel is used, but one can also use a *"comb"* (figure 262 BELOW), a sort of stone axe with teeth. The teeth are a set of metal spikes or needles, pointed at both ends and about 1 cm thick. These are locked into place by a metal wedge, which can easily be removed when it is time to take them to the blacksmith for reforging.

Figure 262.

Figure 263.

152

The finish is usually done with a wide chisel (figure 263), whose cutting edge can be 12 cm wide or more.

During several months, I had the experience of working in Alsace. The stone dulled my tools so quickly that I was obliged to have two sets. Each evening after the day's work, I took the tools used that day, now quite blunted, to the smith. He reforged and retempered them during the next day, while I worked with my alternate set of tools. These I brought to him at the end of the day, and picked up my newly forged set; and so on. Since the mid-twentieth century, chisels can be made with a more durable blade of tungsten folded into the iron, serving as the cutting edge.

The Particularities of Shale

Shale is often trimmed on its edges when used in rather thin plates (1 to 4 cm) as roofing material. Striking the large, flat face of the plate will probably result in its breaking in a way not intended. To dress thicker stones, the procedure is similar, that is, by trimming only the edges, where the strata of the stone are visible, and by cutting with the edge of the chisel held approximately perpendicular to the strata. Roofers use a special tool – a trimming hammer, shown here – which is suited to thin stones, but for more substantial thicknesses, the stonecutter will use a flat ended chisel about 20-25 mm wide. He must be careful to avoid placing the chisel's cutting edge parallel to the strata, as such a blow would probably split the stone open.

Figure 264. Slater's tools: The bottom tool is stuck into the roofing boards and the slate to be trimmed is set on it precisely along the line where the stone is to be trimmed. This is then done with the sharp edge of the cutting tool, above. The cutting tool also doubles as a hammer (the right end in the photo) and as a nail-puller. The pointed end is for punching holes in the slate.

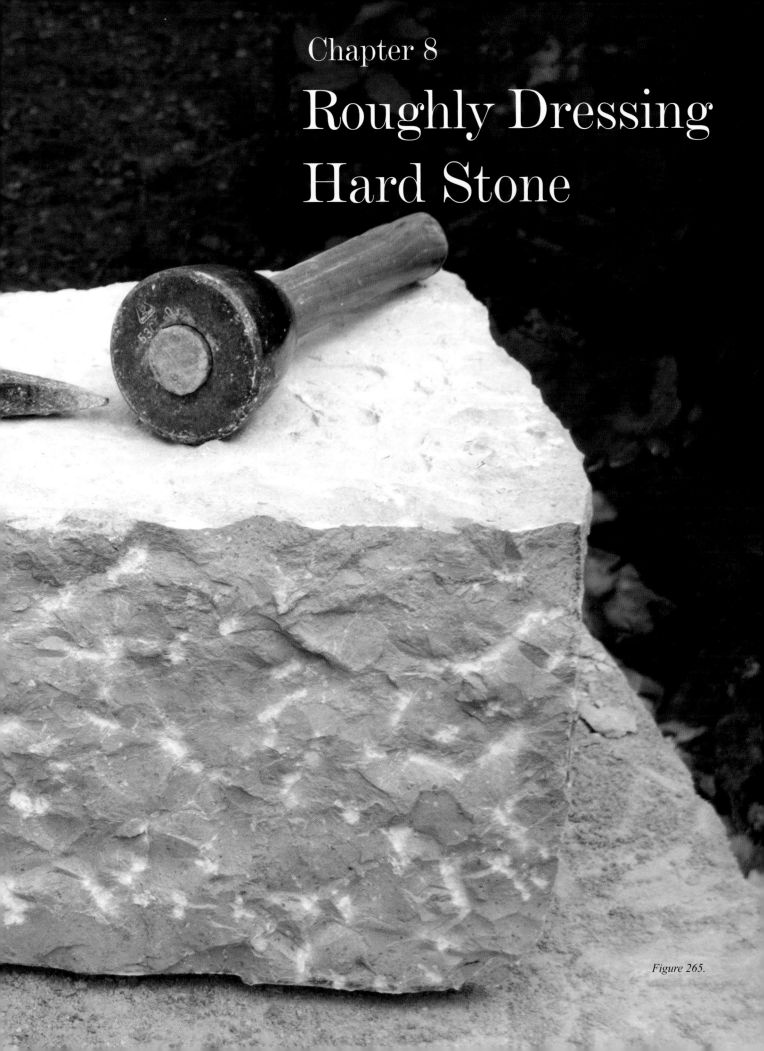

Chapter 8
Roughly Dressing Hard Stone

Figure 265.

Roughly Dressing Hard Stone

Often, a building is made partly or entirely of stones dressed only roughly (as in figures 259 and 261). The joints will be about 10 mm thick, but whatever the thickness chosen, the mason tries to maintain it throughout.

For works to be assembled with joints of 10 mm, the stones will be cut to a tolerance of not more than 5 mm, because the imprecisions between two stones may compound to total 10 mm. For any joints which do not of themselves open as far as 10 mm, a little additional mortar on the inside of the joint will maintain the regularity of the ensemble.

Rough dressing is particularly used with hard stones; for soft stones, it is scarcely longer nor more difficult to dress them more precisely to within a tolerance of 3 mm. (More precision than this does, however, require more care and thus more time; the method will be given in the next chapter.)

Figure 266.

A quick look at the stone will reveal which side is best to present as the visible face, and this is usually dressed first.

Dressing a stone always implies two major steps:

- **Trim the entire periphery (the four edges) of the face, then**
- **Reduce the mass remaining in the middle until it reaches the level of the periphery.**

First Step

Figure 267.   *Figure 268.*

Turn the stone, or position yourself in relation to it, in such a way that you can draw a line defining the edge of the face to be cut. This must pass below any holes, hollows, or chips in the stone so that they will be eliminated when the face is dressed.

Figure 269.

Figure 270.

Trim the edge along the trait using the pitching chisel.

Figure 271.

Figure 272. 1

Turn the stone again, or else, go to the other side. Place a straight edged rule along the edge previously trimmed; If this is not sufficiently flat that the edge lies along it (within the 5 mm or whatever tolerances of imprecision that you have decided to accept), trim it more precisely with an ordinary (flat-edged) chisel. On the opposite side, align another rule parallel to the first one, and trace another trait along it (**1**). If the first rule cannot stay in place by itself, have someone else hold it for a few moments.

The extremities of the two previous traits should then be joined across the stone (**2**).

Then, with a rule placed along the line just traced, draw the parallel line on the opposite side of the stone using the method of the two parallel rules (**3**). (This is described and illustrated more fully in the next chapter; see especially figures 298, 300, 302, and 333.)

When this is done, you will have the outline of the periphery of the face to be dressed. This must then be trimmed with the pitching chisel, and perhaps also with the flat chisel if more precision is needed.

Because you were careful to align the two pairs of opposite sides by the method of the parallel rulers when tracing the lines, the four edges, and hence the entire periphery, will all be in the same plane.

Figure 273. 2

Figure 274. 3

Figure 275.

157

Second Step

Using the pointed chisel, chip off (progressively) the mass remaining in the middle until you have reduced it to the same level as the periphery. The face thus dressed will be flat – within the limits of precision that you have decided upon, in most cases between 3 and 7 mm for masonry with joints of 6 to 14 mm. You can do this rough cut methodically in parallel diagonal lines spaced about 2 cm apart, or without apparent method, just relying on your eye and your feeling for the stone to chip at it wherever and at whatever angle you feel to be the most effective. Nonetheless, you must be very attentive near the edges, and direct your chisel toward the center. The surface will have a chipped appearance.

Figure 276.

Figure 277.

Figure 278.

Caution: When working with hard stone, especially with a pointed chisel, you should wear protective goggles, as small, sharp chips of stone fly unpredictably, whistling as they pass your ears.

For more precise work:

The rough work shown here is unsuitable if you wish your margin of imprecision to be less than 5 mm. In this case, you will have to modify your method somewhat, and take more time and care.

On the periphery: Instead of just a rough trim of the periphery with the pitching chisel, you will follow this up with a more precise trim, to within a tolerance of only one or two mm, with a flat chisel, 20 to 30 mm wide.

On the finished surface: As your periphery is now more flat and precise, so must the inside be reduced more precisely to arrive at the same level. After a rough dressing with the pointed chisel, you can refine this with a further passage, or even with a ***gradine***, chisel with flat teeth.

Figure 279. These stones have been cut more precisely than the one in the demonstration; consequently the periphery has been chiseled out with a straight-edged chisel. Korčula, Croatia.

Squaring the Stone

Once the face to be placed in the façade is dressed, the stone is completed by roughly cutting its two sides and its top and bottom surfaces to be perpendicular to the face. Each surface is dressed as was outlined above, that is, in two principal steps:

trimming the periphery, and then
reducing the mass in the center to the same level as that of the periphery.

Figure 280. The periphery is marked out with pencil traits. The sides can be done one by one, or, as here, simultaneously. In this case, I have decided to accept a broken edge, scarcely noticeable from in front, because to remove it would involve considerably reducing the stone's visible surface, as well as taking much time to reduce the stone through its entire depth.

Figure 281. Here, the stone has been turned over, and its sides roughly trimmed with the pitching chisel.

Figure 282. The top surface is trimmed along the front.

Figure 283. Then along the sides, perpendicular to the front face.

Figure 284. Once the four edges of the periphery have been trimmed, the mass remaining in the middle is chipped off using the pointed chisel, as explained above, to obtain an acceptably level top surface.

The bottom surface is, in this case, almost within my accepted margin of imprecision naturally—a small retouch (at the bottom left) and the stone is ready to be set in the masonry.

Figure 285. A wall of roughly dressed hard limestone. Korčula, Croatia.

Chapter 9

Dressing a Face and Squaring a Stone with Precision

Figure 286.

Dressing a Face

This demonstration pertains particularly to cutting soft stone, but with the modifications already noted (in Chapter 7) it is also applicable to cutting hard stone.

Figure 287.

This irregularly-shaped stone has been salvaged from a rock pile and split up to be of manageable size (hence the white surfaces). The stonecutter begins by looking at all of its faces to determine which one can best be presented as the visible face, and what shape and dimensions to give it.

As this stone naturally has two large surfaces – those turned toward the observer – already fairly flat and not far from being perpendicular, it lends itself well to becoming a corner stone. Thus, we have this option, which we can use if we wish after dressing the principal face.

Generally, I prefer to start by dressing the surface which I will use as the visible exterior face (or one of these – the largest one – if dealing with a cornerstone). But keep in mind that, for whatever indications I give here, there are always alternative ways of achieving the same result, so adapt your method to whatever works well and makes sense to you as you gain experience.

The dressing of a surface – any flat surface, as well as many rounded ones – can be resumed in two principal steps, already explained on p 156 of the preceding chapter. These are:

trim the periphery(all four edges), and then

reduce the mass left in the middle to the level of the periphery.

162

Figures 288-289.

First, though, I will make a very rough cut to take off any important bumps or protuberances. Although this is not obligatory, such bumps can be troublesome:

— when I turn the stone over to work on another face (for it can swing around in an unexpected way and injure my hands),
— when I am working on the stone (for it may rock or move about),
— when I want to set the ruler against a surface to draw a straight line, as in the next step.

The large sharp-toothed chisel is very efficient for this job (even if one of the teeth is missing), as is the toothed stone ax.

1) Trimming the Periphery

1 A): Mark off and trim the first edge of the periphery.

Figure 290.

Having taken off the bumps likely to be troublesome, I turn the side I wish to dress first upwards. (This is not obligatory once you have understood the method, but proceeding in this way will make the explanation easier to follow.)

Next, using a ruler, I draw a line a bit below the edge; this must be low enough to pass below any holes or depressions in the surface I intend to dress. In this case, there are no holes or depressions, so I can draw my trait very close to the edge.

Figure 291.

Using a chisel, I cut along the line to create a flat surface along the edge, extending two or three centimeters (about an inch) into the stone.

Figure 292.

To avoid breaking pieces off of the edge, I must cut along it **while keeping the outside corner of the chisel slightly outside of the edge,** if only by a few millimeters, while angling the chisel somewhat toward the interior. While advancing along the line, then, the chisel will also go inwards, but before it passes completely inside the edge, I must reposition it on the outside once again. This you will quickly learn to do without interrupting your rhythm.

You can go over the same part of the chiseled band several times as long as you see that you have not yet reached the trait or that your band is still inclined toward the exterior. (It should end up approximately horizontal.) This will also give you the opportunity to reposition the chisel. With each passage, you can incline the chisel a bit more toward the interior, until your band is (approximately) horizontal. Stonecutting, and even more, sculpture, is much a matter of using the suppleness of the wrist.

165

Upon approaching the far end of the edge, I stop, because the chances of breaking off the corner are great. **At the corners, it is necessary to work from the outside toward the inside,** and never the opposite. So I turn the stone around – or go to the other end – and work in the other direction.

Figure 293.

Figure 294.

The result is a level band like this.

I verify that it is perfectly flat by applying the straight edge. In this case, it isn't (if I want to limit my imprecisions to 1 mm, which is the case). Looking carefully, you can see that almost all of the chiseled edge is 2 or 3 mm higher than the ends, with the exception of a few centimeters just to the left of the center portion.

Figure 295.

You can mark the places that are still too high with a pencil if that helps you to visualize them, and then reduce these areas further.

Figure 296.

When you have finished, the ruler should lie flat against the stone along its entire length.

Figure 297.

167

1 B): Mark off and trim the opposite side of the periphery (using the method of the two parallel rulers).

Figure 298.

Leaving the ruler or straight edge in place, go to the opposite side of the stone and place another ruler against that face near the top, adjusting its alignment so that it is parallel to the first one. To facilitate this alignment, the two rulers should be long enough to protrude beyond the stone on both ends, and you must lean back far enough that you can see both of the protruding parts simultaneously. When you have adjusted the second ruler so that it is visibly parallel with the first, use it to mark a corresponding line. This line, like the first one, must pass beneath any holes or depressions in the face to be dressed.

Figure 299.

Cut along this new line as you did on the opposite side, to obtain a second level band. But this time, when you check it with the straight edge for flatness, verify also (using the two rules) that the two edges are parallel. If this is not the case, adjust one or the other (or both).

Figure 300.

1 C): Mark off and trim the remaining two sides of the periphery.

Figure 301.

Figure 302.

Next, go to each of the two remaining edges, and draw lines joining the ends of the two level bands just created. You can leave the two straight edges in place to do this, or simply join the two level bands by eye.

When you have cut along these traits on each end, you will see, if all is well, that this second pair of level bands is also parallel.

2): Reduce the mass left in the middle to the level of the periphery.

Figure 303.

Figure 304.

You now have the four edges of the periphery all in the same plane, which will be that of the face when it is finished. In the middle remains a mass that you must cut down to this same plane. With soft stone, this is best done with a chisel with large pointed teeth. But if this tool is not available to you, others, such as the pointed chisel, or a fine-toothed chisel, or even an ordinary straight-edged all metal chisel will do. Wooden handles, though, are likely to break under the mallet blows, which will be a lot more forceful than in the previous step.

To reduce this mass, work from the edges or the angles toward the middle. Attack the mass at its base (less 1 mm, so as not to dig in too deeply) and try to maintain your newly created surface as close as possible to the required finished level – that of the periphery – as you advance. Usually, beginners tend to be overly cautious and take off too little material, producing a rough cut where the surface rises from the periphery toward the center that must be reworked (often, several times). Going almost directly to the required finished level right from the start will greatly improve your efficiency. Practice this on surfaces which will be buried in the masonry; with these, you risk nothing should you chance to take off too much.

Figure 305.   *Figure 306.*   *Figure 307.*

CAUTION: When you arrive near the middle, however, and there remains only a small mound of material to take off, go about this more delicately; instead of working at the base as you did up until this point, take off the small remaining part in two or three steps. Otherwise, when there is hardly any mass behind the point at which you are working, the last piece may break off more deeply than you expected, gouging out a hole in the finished surface. Again, you can experiment with this with no danger on surfaces that will be hidden in the masonry (top and bottom, particularly); you will soon discover the limits beyond which you must be especially cautious.

The surface is usually finished with a stone axe, but can also be done with a mallet, preferably wooden (see Figure 263), and a wide chisel. These are usually easier to handle for beginners, but the stone axe is more efficient once you have gotten used to it.

Figure 309.

Figure 308.

Figure 310.

Figure 311.

Figure 312.

I prefer working from opposite corners (two, or sometimes all four) toward the center.

Here again, when arriving at the last small band to be removed, do this more cautiously and progressively to avoid seeing the last piece break off too deeply.

Here is the finished face. You can place the straight edge against it anywhere, including diagonally; it will be perfectly level.

Figure 313.

In a wall with irregular joints, your stone is now ready to set. In fact, the work done according to the above directives is probably excessively precise in such cases. The stones could be cut more roughly, in half the time, by giving harder blows with the stone axe and spacing these a bit further apart; and also by accepting less precision (e.g. tolerances of 4 mm instead of 1) for the periphery, if this corresponds to what is done in the surrounding masonry.

Figure 314.

Squaring a Stone

But if you intend to square your stones, there is still much to do. In this day and age, this is rarely done manually, because almost all stones suitable for cutting are bought at the quarries mechanically sawed and squared, usually to the dimensions ordered by the client, at little or no more extra cost, and stones sold rough (field stones) are usually too small to reduce by cutting, or too hard. Even an adept of handwork, like myself, will not square up large quantities of stones. But as I don't like a machine finish, I will always recut, with hand tools, whatever surfaces will be visible in the finished work.

In any case, the method is good to know, and comes in handy here and there, when you don't have a big series to do.

The Upper (or Lower) Surface:

Figure 315.

There may be several possibilities at this stage. I must now choose a height for my stone, the height being the distance between the upper and the lower surfaces. But, if the stone is smaller at one end, or if it has any broken edges – both of which are probable – then increasing the height probably implies decreasing the stone's useable length. In this case, because of the piece missing at the lower left, the more I displace my lower trait toward the bottom to increase the height, the more I have to push the vertical trait toward the right, which shortens the length. I have opted for the compromise that is now marked on the stone. You may have the impression, viewing it from this angle, that I could have drawn the upper trait one or two cm higher still; but in fact, the stone is thinner behind – you will see this when we dress the other surfaces – and does not provide the volume necessary for such a height.

Once I have determined my top and bottom limits for the face, then, I must mark them off on the sides of the stone. These are lines 3 and 4 seen above, and they must be precisely *square with* (i.e. perpendicular to) the already cut face, and meet the top and bottom traits (1 and 2).

These lines should be drawn using a square, one side of which will be set against the face as shown here and on the following page. (Figures 316, 318, and 319.)

Figure 316.

173

To dress the top (or bottom), I will apply the general procedure outlined for dressing any face, with one exception which we will soon see.

The first edge of the periphery

Returning to the front of the stone, I cut a level band, forming the edge of the face, using the methods explained earlier (pp.164-166).

Figure 317.

The opposite edge of the periphery

According to the procedure I outlined above, I should now trace and cut a level band on the opposite (back) side, using the method of the two parallel rules. But if this back end is sloping off – which happens often, and is quite permissible, as this part will buried in the masonry – then I will have no surface on which to place my rule or trace my line. So I will skip this step and do the two side surfaces directly.

Figure 318.

Figure 319.

The two sides edges of the periphery

I verify that my traits on the sides (3 and 4 in the photo on the preceding page) are **square with the face**. This is primordial for creating the top and bottom surfaces for ashlars.

I cut along the traits on the sides, and verify that the chiseled band thus created is level, **and** is also square with the face.

174

Reduce the mass left in the middle to the level of the periphery

Figure 320.

Figure 321.

I take off the mass in the middle.

You can see in this photo how the stone slopes toward the opposite side and toward the rear; so my flat surface will not extend right to the stone's far edges. But as you can see in the finished stone *AT BOTTOM*, even though there is a piece missing from the top surface (which will be buried in the masonry, and thus, not visible), there remains enough level surface to furnish a support for the stone which will later be set on top.

Once this surface has been rough cut, I finish it, starting from the corners. At these places, it is easy to see if the surface being cut is really level, because you are working between two level bands that are only a few centimeters apart. But if you feel the need, you can also check with a straight edge. You will work from two (or from all four) corners toward the middle.

Figure 322.

If you wish, *one option* (once you are well away from the corner) is to jump 5 or 10 cm ahead, and level out a band a few centimetres wide and at the same level as the periphery (and thus, as the finished surface). This can serve as a guide to maintaining the work on this face at the desired level. From this band, you can work forwards (from right to left if you are holding the axe with your right hand at the ax head), or backwards.

When you have finished, the top surface will be square with the face. A few holes, chips, or depressions in the upper or lower surfaces are of no consequence – unless they are in the edge that meets the face – as these surfaces are hidden in the masonry. As for the part that slopes off toward the rear, which you can also see in the inset photo of the block before it was worked (Figure 324), this is also of no consequence as long as there is sufficient flat surface to receive and support another stone, even with the help of some shims. I could have eliminated this minor flaw by drawing my top trait lower, but this would have reduced the height of my stone by 3 cm. I prefer, in this case, to accept the hollow in the top surface. This kind of decision can be made right from the start, when you examine the stone to decide how to use it and what dimensions to give it.

Figure 323.

Figure 324.

If I have no good lateral face permitting me to make a cornerstone, I will then cut the bottom surface square with the front face. But in the event – as here – that the stone is suitable for a corner, I will cut it now.

The Second Face of the Cornerstone

I choose to deal first with the second face of the corner, because the traits can be drawn on surfaces already dressed, and this is easier than trying to draw straight lines on an irregular surface. Once I have dressed this side, the bottom surface will in turn be easier to mark off.

Figure 325.   *Figure 326.*   *Figure 327.*

The traits for the second corner face must be drawn square with the face already dressed, as can be seen in the accompanying photos. In this case, a vertical trait had already been drawn to help visualize the preceding step; but its accuracy should now be verified. (Figure 325.)

Figure 328.

Figure 329.

Figure 330.

Figure 331.

The pitching chisel is the best tool to use when beginning a rough cut *on traits drawn on a level surface.* When positioned as shown in the upper right photo, it allows you to easily knock off large pieces.

CAUTION: At the corners, position the pitching chisel so that part of its edge extends beyond the stone (ABOVE RIGHT). Also, when you have more than about six cm to take off, it is prudent to do this in two stages; only on the second should you approach the trait.

176

Cut the two edges just drawn. The rough cut (trim) is done, as just explained, with the pitching chisel, the more precise leveling with a straight-edged chisel of 25-30 mm, as before. Verify that the chiseled bands are indeed level, and are square with the face already cut.

Figure 332.

Figure 333.

Mark off the other two edges using the method of the two parallel rulers, as before. Cut them, and then the entire face, as you have learned to do.

The finished surface will, of course, be square with the others, and two rules placed anywhere on it will be parallel.

Figure 334.

Only the bottom surface now remains; as promised, it is easy to mark off, as the traits are drawn on surfaces already leveled. Be sure to draw your traits so that they pass beneath any and all important hollows or holes, so as to exclude them from the finished surface.

Figure 335.

Figure 336.

Cut the surface as you have done with the others: first, establish the periphery, and then, reduce the mass remaining in the middle.

Figure 337.

178

The last surfaces remaining to retouch are the sides. If, in fact, the corner stone will be inserted in a wall which is otherwise made of uncut fieldstones, the sides need not be cut, for they adjoin similarly uncut stones with equally irregular joints. But if the stone is to juxtapose others cut with the same precision, then you must dress the edges to be perfectly vertical. As the remainder of these surfaces will be inside the masonry, they can be dressed only roughly. Hollows are of no importance on the inside faces, but there must be nothing protruding, so that the adjacent stone can be fitted tightly.

Figure 338.

Figure 339.

179

DAVID CAMPBELL

ARCHITECTURES
INSOLITES

mail: etherealcastles@yahoo.com
site: www.archimad-boss.com

Chapter 10
Making an Arch

Figure 340.

Making an Arch

In the chapter **Arches**, we have seen the theoretical aspects of drawing different forms of arches; here, we will see how to put this theory into practice, using a semicircular arch as an example.

Drawing the Form and the Template

As discussed earlier (Chapter 4), the arch stones are set up on a form, usually built of wood, made to correspond to the real size of the arch's intrados (less a few centimeters if you wish to set the stones on shims; this possibility will be discussed later).

As for cutting the arch stones, you will need to make a template, corresponding to the stone's real size, to ensure the uniformity of the curve. The outlines of the form and of the template are often drawn at the same time, as they require the same setup of materials.

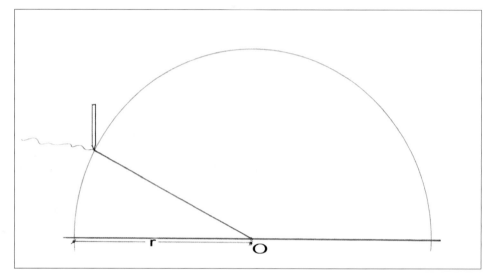

Figure 341.

There are several possible ways of proceeding; I usually do the following:

Draw a straight line A (the base line), using a long ruler or straight edge. In modern times, this can be done directly on a sheet of plywood which will then be cut out with a jigsaw; in the Middle Ages (and earlier) the form was made by assembling a series of boards on which the curve was drawn. (See the following page.)

—position a nail to be the center **O**.
—make a loop at the end of a cord (which must not be stretchable); place it around the nail.
—position a pencil on the cord, at precisely the required radius, with the cord wound once or twice around it just above the pencil point; hold the cord on the pencil with a finger while drawing.
—taking care to maintain the pencil always vertical and the cord taut, draw the semicircle of the required radius; this will correspond to the intrados.

Figure 342.

For the Form: Cut out the plywood or the boards. The semicircle must, in fact, be drawn and cut out twice, and one panel applied to each side of a wooden frame; this gives two-point support to the stones being set upon it. But when assembling the two sides of the framework, be careful to align them perfectly, without swiveling either one the slightest bit. Unless you are a very accomplished carpenter, then, I advise nailing the boards on the frame before marking them. It is perhaps easiest to draw the semicircle on a piece of Bristol board, which you will then cut out to transfer the drawing on to the wooden form; or to draw directly on a piece of plywood. During the Middle Ages, the forms were made by skilled carpenters, and not by the masons – at least, on the more important building sites.

Figure 343. Two forms, showing different ways of disposing the boards on the frame.

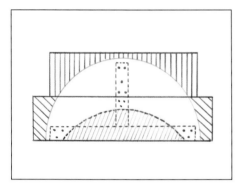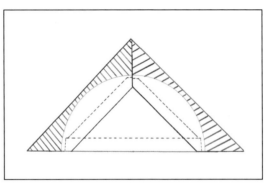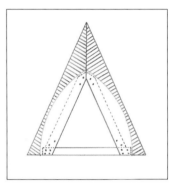

Figures 344-345. Two ways of assembling a semicircular form.

Figure 346. Sketch for assembling a pointed form. The parts with the oblique lines will be cut out.

For the template: This will be scarcely bigger than the biggest of the stones you will use for the arch, so you need only draw a portion of the intrados – plus the corresponding portion of the extrados. You should also draw several possible positions for the joints, which will be straight lines drawn from the center (O in the above sketch). With this choice of joints marked on your template, it can be used for marking any and all of your arch stones by choosing the joint, which allows you to use the maximum volume available for each block.

Figure 347. The photo shows the template that will be used in the following demonstration. The joint M (for Moyen, average) represents the normal size to which the stones would be cut to have 7 equal pieces. This number is arbitrary, but was chosen to give stones of a size convenient both practically and esthetically. M + 1, M+2, M+ 3 and M -1, M-2, M-3 correspond to the number of centimeters more or less than the average (M), measured along the intrados. This system also allows you to quickly calculate, when some of your stones are done, the length which you still need to complete your arch.

183

Marking the Arch Stones

In principle, arch stones are planned so that their strata are perpendicular to the intrados, as though radiating from the center. (This is an approximation, of course, as the intrados is a curve.) This is done both for structural and for esthetic considerations. But when the strata are not noticeable, this is of little importance, and the stonecutter can give the impression of the arch radiating around the center by leaving the marks of the stone axe in radiating lines when finishing the surfaces, as in figure 340.

The template can be placed in one of two ways, as you choose:

1) with one side on the edge of the block (fig. 348), or
2) centered between the two sides of the block.

The advantage of 2) is that the strata, when they are visible, are more symmetrical around the center, giving a strong radiating impression; the disadvantage is that you must cut both sides, instead of taking advantage of the side of the block which is already dressed. When the strata are well marked, I always choose option **2)**; and that is what I will do here, even though the strata are scarcely visible.

Figure 348.

If you opt for position 2), then, place your template with its two corners (one of which you will have to designate from among your several possible joints) touching the edge in which you will cut the intrados. Draw your traits against the edges of the template. As I wish to use as much as possible of the block's volume, I opt for joint M+1, which just fits in, M+2 falling slightly outside of the limits of the stone.

Figure 349.

The resulting traits are seen here. As it was not possible to mark M+1 with the template in position, I have made a small mark at each of its extremities, which I will now join using a straight edge.

Figure 350.

184

At each of the points where the corners of the template, as you placed it previously, meet the stone's edge, make two small vertical marks. From each of these points, draw, using a square, a vertical line, which will be perpendicular to (i.e. – square with) the face upon which you have outlined the arch stone. In principle, one uses the inside edges of the square, but if you have checked that the outside edges are parallel with these, you can use them instead; I find that this enables me to better see my guide points.

Figure 351. Perpendicular traits representing the limits of the intrados.

Extend the traits representing the joints beyond the extrados so that they reach an edge of the stone. Depending on the curve and the dimensions of the block, this may be the end where you will cut the extrados, or it may be one of the sides, as in this photo. Starting from each of these guide points on the edges, drop a trait, using the square, perpendicular to the face. These represent the side limits of the archstone, where there will be a joint between stones.

Figure 352. Perpendicular trait drawn where the joint meets the edge of the stone.

Figure 353.

Turn the block over.

Figure 354.

Find the points where your perpendicular traits representing the limits of the intrados meet the edge of what is now the top face, and position the template precisely on these points (or half a mm further in, to allow for the thickness of the pencil trait). Draw the outline of the arch stone. Don't forget that you have opted to use M+1 for this stone, so it must be used on both sides; it is, moreover, the only one which falls correctly on your guide lines or points. As on the other side, you can only mark a guide point at the upper end (extrados), and draw the trait after removing the template.

Figure 355.

Extend the lines representing the joints beyond the extrados, as you did on the opposite face. These extended traits should meet, on the edge of the block, those perpendicular traits that you drew previously. In these places, you can accept some small imprecision, though (2, even 3 mm), as you are working with surfaces that will be hidden in the masonry.

Figure 356.

You now have the outlines of your arch stone on the front and on the back faces of the block; your perpendicular traits have allowed you to align the same outline on the two opposite faces.

ATTENTION: *Your block must be perfectly square before you mark any traits; otherwise, your perpendicular traits will not be perpendicular to both faces and the stone will be twisted.*

Also, this demonstration presupposes that you have cut all of your stones to the same depth – that which you have chosen for the ensemble.

Cutting the stones

The different surfaces can be done in the order you choose; usually the sides are done first. There is some difference of opinion as to whether it is best next to do the intrados or the extrados; my preference is to leave the intrados for the last, working on it while the block rests on the rounded extrados (which I block with wedges), rather than working last on the extrados while the stone rests on the finished, fragile edges of the intrados. In this demonstration, I will follow this preference.

The Sides (the joints), as with all flat surfaces, are cut as explained previously:

1) **Trim the periphery** by chiseling around the four edges. You can check your traits by the method of the two parallel rulers, but this is superfluous; if the outline is correct, which will already be evident if the two faces can be joined by perpendicular traits along the sides (fig. 356), then the rulers *must* be parallel.

Figure 357. Rough cut with the pitching chisel along the outline of the periphery.

2) **Reduce the mass left in the middle to the level of the periphery.** Here, because the surface in question is a joint to be filled with mortar, you can take the risk of digging too deeply in order to work quickly; this will be of no consequence as long as you don't chip the edges. On the other hand, leaving any areas higher than the level of the periphery will prevent adjoining stones from fitting tightly together.

Figure 358. The outline Chiseled precisely.

Figure 360. The inside surface finished with the stone axe.

Figure 359. Rough cut on the side, with the toothed chisel.

187

The Extrados: The extrados is already marked on the front and back faces. When you join these traits across the two sides that you have just cut, then you will have outlined the perimeter of the extrados. These traits will be perpendicular to the front and back faces if there is no error; check with the square before proceeding.

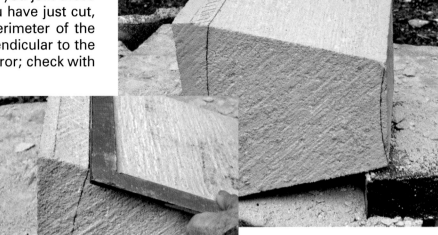

Figure 362.

Figure 361.

To cut the extrados, you will follow the method already explained – chisel around the periphery, then reduce the mass in the middle to the level of the periphery – with one difference: here, you are dealing with a curved surface. Consequently, the peripheral band chiseled along the curves cannot be verified with a straight edge, but rather, by the application of a ***counter-profile***. In this case, this will be the concave curve at the limit of the extrados, which you cut out of the Bristol board when you cut out your template. You should use this counter-profile to check the curve, particularly along the edges, and can also use it at different stages of dressing the middle parts; most often, though, you will verify the work with a straight edge applied in a back to front direction, which will always be a series of straight lines. For finishing this surface, then, you have two methods of verification, one for each of your two planes.

Here, as for the sides, the surface (with the exception of the edges) will be buried in the masonry, and you can practice improving your rapidity and efficiency without risk if you chance to go too deeply.

Figure 363. Chiseled band along a straight line.

Figure 364. Chiseled band along a curve.

Figure 365. From back to front, the verification is done with a straight edge, ...

Figure 366. ... whereas along the curve, the verification is done with a counter-profile

188

The Intrados

For this, you proceed in the same manner as for the extrados, except that, the intrados being a concave surface, you must verify its exactitude with a convex counter-profile. Keep in mind also that this surface, unlike the extrados, will be entirely visible, so there is no room for error. Nonetheless, with practice (which you can acquire especially on the inside joints and other non-visible surfaces like the extrados), you can learn to rough-cut rapidly and precisely with the toothed chisel to within 1 to 4 mm of your final level, which you will then finish with a stone axe or with a wide chisel.

Figure 367. Chiseled bands around the periphery.

Figure 368. Rough cut with the toothed chisel.

*Figure 369. Finish work with the stone axe, or as here, with a wide chisel **only in the direction shown**; verification will be done with a straight edge applied in the same direction.*

Figure 370. In the other direction, verification is done with the counter-profile.

Setting the Stones on the Form

It is helpful – at least until you have gained a certain experience – to set up your arch stones on the form, or on a life-size drawing on a level surface, as soon as you have finished several stones. This enables you to ensure that the stones fit together at the joints as expected, with an unbroken curve on the intrados. (Check this with the counter-profile of the intrados overlapping two adjacent stones.) Also, when you come to the last stone to be cut, you can verify the dimensions required, and cut it accordingly. When the stones are set up with shims and wedges, as will be necessary (details follow), the theoretical cut may have to be modified slightly in practice.

The Uniformity of the Joints: An arch can be set up *dry* (without mortar), but it is customary to fill the joints with lime mortar; this allows the ensemble to adjust to minor shifting without breakage. If you are working with joints of only 2 or 3 mm, you can only fill them by pouring liquid mortar, made without sand, into the joints from above, once the arch is completely assembled on the form. The space for the joints must be taken into consideration when cutting the stones, either by taking off 2 or 3 mm more from one side of each stone than is shown in your theoretical drawing, or by catching up the difference on the last stone to be cut.

When you set your arch stones on the form, then, use shims – all of the same thickness – in the joints to maintain the desired distance between them. In some places you will also have to use wedges, as will be explained below.

Figure 371.

Set up the stones on each side of the form, from the bottom toward the summit. Make sure that the distance between the springing stones at each end really corresponds to what was planned in the theoretical drawing, and be sure that their faces are perfectly aligned by applying a straight edge sufficiently long. As you add stones, be sure to control the alignment of their faces in two dimensions – vertical (or at least, oblique), and horizontal. The horizontal alignment must be verified across the open space between the two sides.

Figure 372.

Figure 373.

Figure 374.

If the intrados doesn't fit perfectly on the form, trust the cut of your stones rather than the form – especially if you are a competent stonecutter, but a mediocre carpenter. Don't forget that the form's function is solely to temporarily support the stones, and, although it can be used as a guide, this is not its role. The slightest misalignment between the two portions of the form (front and back) will influence the position of the stone placed upon it, and you must be ready to make adjustments with shims and wedges as required to maintain the regularity of your intrados and the alignment of the faces. Verify the curve of the intrados by applying the counter-profile across each adjoining pair of stones. Where necessary, adjust the stones in relation to the form with small wedges, pushing these in as far as required, here to incline a stone, there to open up a joint. You will not necessarily make the same adjustment on the back side of the form that you made in front, and vice-versa.

Figure 375.

When all are in place except the last stone (the **keystone**, which occupies the summit), apply the template with one edge against the second last stone, to see exactly where to cut the key. This may not be exactly where you had expected after your theoretical calculation, but adjust as necessary, taking into account also the space for the joint at each side. It is even possible that there may be a break in the intrados if a joint is too, or not sufficiently, inclined; you can compensate by ignoring the joints on your template, finding a position for it in which the intrados fills the gap correctly, and mark the joints necessary for that position on the template. You will then use these to cut the keystone or adjust the one already prepared, if you have previously cut it. Remember, though, that this montage is just a trial run. When the arch is set up *in situ* (on site) for its permanent incorporation in the building, there may be other small shifts in position, so it is prudent to leave a small margin on the keystone, part or all of which can be removed as necessary in situ to make a perfect fit.

Alternatively, you may simply cut all the stones according to your theoretical drawing, and adjust the ensemble directly on the form *in situ*, doing whatever is necessary, with wedges and shims, to make it fit. This is, moreover, what happens when the stonecutters furnish the stones to a team of masons who set up the arch on the site. The drawback of this method is that if you, or they, have not correctly estimated the width of the joints or whatever adjustments may be needed to compensate imperfections in the form, it may be necessary, upon reaching the summit, to take down some or all of the stones and reset them.

Figure 376.

Setting up the arch *in situ*.

A few little tricks will help to avoid many of the annoyances you may otherwise have.

For setting the form in place and removing it after use:

If the form rests on an abacus or an impost (see photo), you may have a lot of trouble removing it once the stones are on it. And while hitting it with a hammer may shake it loose, it will also shake loose the stones that you have so laboriously set and sealed. There are two (or perhaps even more) ways of avoiding this problem:

Figure 377.

1) Make the form smaller, cutting it to a radius reduced by several centimeters. (Let us say **"X"**.) Position each stone on the form using shims corresponding in height to **X**. When the stones are set and the mortar has hardened, you can remove the shims one by one to liberate the form. This practice can also help solve the problem of the mortar's leaking out, which we will discuss below.

2) Alternatively, remove 2 (or any convenient number) cm along the bottom of the form – or rather, build your form with 2 cm lacking on the bottom. Place the form on shims of 2 cm at each end, with some sand beneath them. This is what has been done for the above demonstration and in the above photo, where you can distinguish the shims under the ends of the form. These will not

be difficult to remove when the time comes to take down the form.

Whatever solution you adopt, and unless the form is light in relation to the thickness of its supporting stones (which is the case in the above photo), shore up the form with supports which take most of the weight; don't let a heavy form bearing heavy stones weigh down on a fragile support. Modern **mason's stays** (supports) can be extended or retracted millimeter by millimeter; a medieval technique for finely adjusting the height of the form would be to insert two large wedges, thin end overlapping thin end, beneath each stay, and drive them in as much as required, one atop the other, with a mallet.

For pouring the joints:

Traditionally, a goosefoot is carved into the inside of the joints of each arch stone. These must all be of identical form and dimensions (within about half a centimeter), so that when they are filled, the hardened mortar mass blocks any possible movement of the stones in a backwards-forwards direction. To ensure the uniformity of the pattern and of its positioning, you can measure and mark each stone, or, more simply, make a template to apply against the sides of each stone.

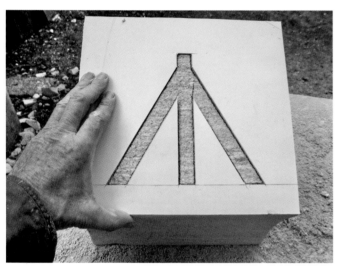

Figure 378.

Figure 379.

At the top of each goosefoot, on the extrados, the entrance hole can be cut in a funnel shape; the liquid mortar will be poured into this hole and will fill the goosefoot and the joint (assuming it is sufficiently thin and runny). At the summit, the mortar can be poured from any kind of container; towards the bottom, where the joints are only slightly inclined, it is easier to introduce a flexible tube into the hole, and pour the mortar into the tube using a funnel.

The mortar is made by simply dissolving the lime powder in a bucket of water. For a half bucket (of about 10 liters), you will need about a dozen trowels full of powdered lime, which you stir to dissolve at each addition. Add more if it still seems too runny. The mortar should be thin enough – like a French *crêpe* batter – to enter a joint only 2 mm wide, but with larger joints, it can be thicker, more like an American pancake batter.

For sealing the joints

Before pouring mortar into the joints, they must be sealed on all sides, leaving only the top open, so that the mortar does not run out again. To this purpose, you must make a thick mortar of lime mixed with sand of a suitable color, as these joints will be visible in the finished work. Cover the joints completely with this mortar, pushing it in with the trowel edge at least several millimeters. Let it start to set a bit before pouring the liquid mortar (about 15 minutes; longer for thicker joints). It is easy to seal the joints on the front and back faces, but those on the intrados are hard to reach, if the stones are set directly against the form. Two solutions (or perhaps more) are possible:

As proposed above, you can construct your form with a somewhat shorter radius, and set the stones on shims. If these are about 5 cm high, you can pass a gloved hand between the stones and the form to apply the mortar to the joints.

Alternatively, rather than placing wooden shims between the stones to keep the joint open, use instead a strip of cardboard of the required thickness across the bottom of the joints, as you see in these photos (BELOW). The cardboard must not contain any compressible alveoli, and the strips should be a bit longer than the thickness of the arch. They will serve as shims to maintain the joint open to the thickness you have chosen for the cardboard, and will also prevent the mortar from running out. Although water will probably seep through, the thicker mortar will not.

Figure 380.

Figure 381.

When pouring liquid mortar, be sure to have a supply of thick mortar at hand to quickly seal off any leaks as soon as they appear. Thicken the liquid mortar if necessary, but not so much that it won't run into the spaces it is intended to fill.

You may even find, when setting an element in or on a wall, that the mortar runs out through the bottom and into the wall, passing through crevasses in the masonry to finally run out 5 m (or more) further down. If this happens, you must pour in increasingly thicker mortars until the leak through the wall is sealed. Then you can resume filling your intended work with liquid mortar. Avoid this problem by sealing off such possible holes before setting up the elements into which the liquid mortar must be poured.

Figure 382.

Figure 383.

You can help the mortar to fill the joint by inserting a thin ruler or something similar, and agitating it to unblock any places which may be blocked. When the joint is almost full, you will see the mortar level rising inside—pour until it reaches the top. If the joint to be filled is horizontal or on only a slight slope, you can fill it by pouring the mortar into a funnel with a plastic tube attached to one end and the other end leading into the joint.

An hour or so after pouring, when the sealing mortar has set somewhat but and before it can harden, brush off all the excess mortar on the faces with a stiff brush, without scraping it out of the joints.

When the form is taken down (after a few days for small works, or several weeks for important ones), you can take out the cardboard strips by pulling on the protruding ends. If these tear off without the rest coming out, you can reduce what is left with a handsaw inserted in the joint. The joint can then be sealed with mortar, but this is of no structural importance.

Chapter 11
Moldings

Figure 384

Moldings

There are four basic forms of moldings; each of these can be used alone, or in combination with others to make a complex molding which is likely to be more striking.
The basic forms are:

The **_chamfer_**, which is an oblique surface cut between two perpendicular surfaces,

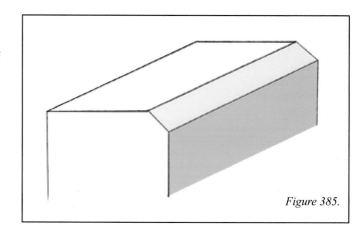

Figure 385.

the **_carderon_**, which is a convex curve corresponding to a quarter of a circle,

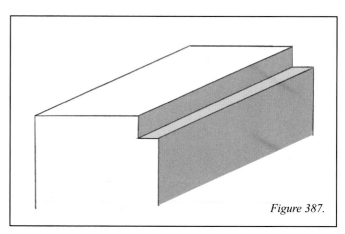

Figure 386.

the **_rabbet_**, which is a right angle,

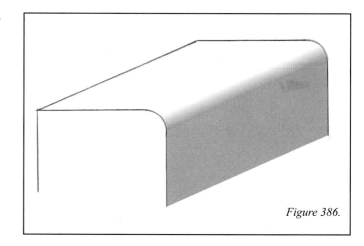

Figure 387.

the **_cavet,_** which is a concave curve corresponding to a quarter of a circle.

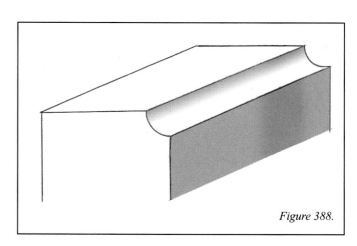

Figure 388.

The chamfer being the easiest to execute, we will deal with it first.

The outlines of the chamfer are drawn on the block, from one end to the other. The measurements are whatever you decide, so AA1 need not be the same distance from the edge as is BB1.

ATTENTION: The indications given in these demonstrations assume that the blocks have been squared precisely before marking.

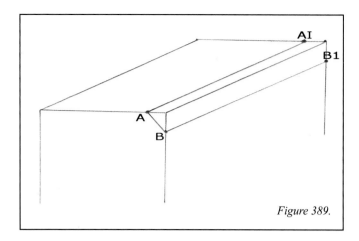

Figure 389.

Start at each end by ***pitching*** (knocking off big pieces by sharp blows to the edge) with a normal or a medium-wide chisel (**1, 2**). This can also be done with a pitching chisel, but on small surfaces such as these, the standard straight-edged chisel is more precise. Continue by chiseling precisely along the end trait and the beginning of the side traits to define the chamfer at both ends (**3**).

If the chamfer is narrow, you can finish it in just two passages; the first a rough cut along the whole length of the stone, approaching fairly close to the side traits (**3**); and a second one to finish the surface, touching the two side traits simultaneously (**4**). The chisel used for this second passage should be a bit wider than the chamfer. (See the following photos.)

Figure 390. 1

Figure 391. 2

Figure 392. 3

Figure 393. 4

If the chamfer is wider than 5 or 6 cm, you should proceed instead as with any other flat surface, that is:

    chisel along the periphery, and
    reduce the mass remaining in the middle to the level of the periphery. This may necessitate several passages.

Verify the work with a straight edge along the length, and with a smaller one across the width of the chamfer.

Figure 394.

The carderon (from the French *quart de rond*, meaning a quarter circle) is done by executing several chamfers, as will be shown.

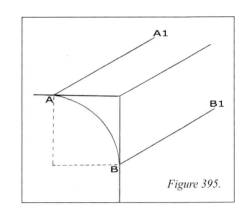

Figure 395.

First, mark the block with the carderon drawn on both ends. AA1 and BB1 represent the beginning and the end of the curve.

Draw CD tangent to the curve at O. If O is the mid-point of the curve, then CX and DX (where X is on the edge) will be equal. This is the most methodical way of proceeding, although not the only one, and I find it easier to deal with a curve when proceeding symmetrically around its mid-point.

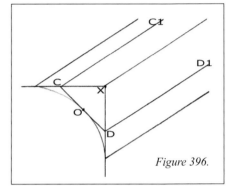

Figure 396.

Cut a chamfer between CC1 and DD1. Verify that the surface is level. The surface in itself has no importance; what we want is the line OO1, because it will be on the surface of the curve to be cut out, and it must be impeccable if the molding is to be straight along its length. And unless your chamfer is impeccable, you cannot count on OO1 being straight.

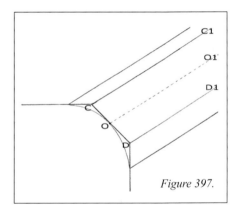

Figure 397.

Next, draw two more chamfers, tangent to the curve at P and at Q. It is best to proceed methodically, as before, maintaining symmetry around the edges and the mid-points. Cutting your two new chamfers will produce two new lines, PP1 and QQ1, which will, like OO1, be on the surface of the curve you wish to produce.

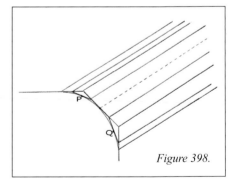

Figure 398.

In theory, you will continue to cut ever smaller chamfers, creating an increasing number of edges with angles less and less abrupt, and you thus approach the curve closer and closer. In practice, you will find that the volumes to remove soon become too insignificant to cut. At this point, it becomes easier to make your smaller chamfers by passing along the edges with a file or with a slab of abrasive stone. You will finish by simply rounding off the numerous remaining edges (be there 4, or 8, or 16) in the same way. Be sure, though, to always work in the direction indicated by the arrows, along the edges and never across them, or the chances are great of your making hollows here and there, spoiling the regularity and the straightness of the molding.

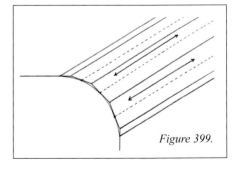

Figure 399.

A special application of the carderon is the column. This is made by applying the carderon to the four edges of the block to produce a cylinder.

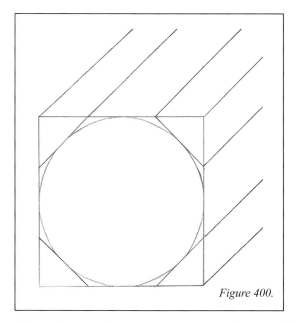

Figure 400.

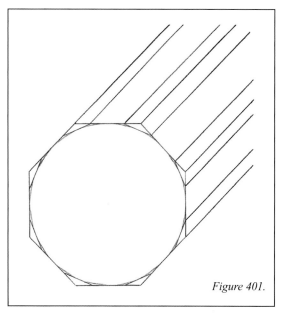

Figure 401.

And so on.

Sometimes columns are octagonal; esthetic considerations aside, this is a time-saver, as the rounding-off process is shortened greatly.

The rabbet: Mark off the rabbet, of the dimensions you require, on both ends of the block. Join these outlines along the length of the stone.

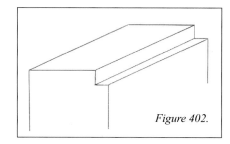

Figure 402.

If the dimensions of the rabbet are important enough that it is not fragile, then you can cut along the lines with a standard chisel. But if the rabbet is narrow, you can easily break off too much material by trying to chisel along a line with the chisel held normally, as in drawing **A**. The fragility increases greatly as the rabbet decreases below 6 cm for a soft stone of compact grain, but this varies with different types of stone; experience will quickly sharpen your judgment.

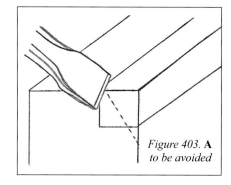

Figure 403. **A** to be avoided

If the dimensions are small, then, you should start by making a rough cut to take off the edge along its whole length, with the chisel – preferably one with pointed teeth – held at an angle like that shown in B, as when cutting a chamfer. Once this is done, you can chisel normally along the lines.

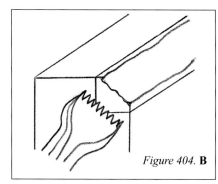

Figure 404. **B**

Cut along each of the two lines. The chisel will block or will break off too much material if held at the vertical, so it is necessary to cut at an angle, and by successive passages, gradually increase this angle to approach the vertical and the horizontal planes. Here again, experience will soon allow you to recognize the limits of what is possible.

Once the vertical and horizontal surfaces are clearly defined, work on the inner corner, first removing excess material with a normal chisel, and then defining and refining it precisely with a wide chisel, to get a neat and well-marked trait.

You can verify that the two surfaces are level with a straight edge. Verify also the squareness of the angle with a small square. This can simply be the corner of a sheet of Bristol board, which you use as a counter-profile.

Figure 405.

Figure 406.

Figure 407.

Figure 408.

Figure 409.

Figure 410.

Figure 411.

202

The cavet: Mark the curve on both ends of the stone. Join AA1 and BB1 along its entire length. These two lines must be parallel to the edge; if they are not, look for and correct the error – probably in the drawing of the curve on one of the ends.

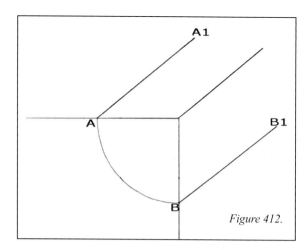

Figure 412.

Do a rough cut as though you were doing a chamfer.

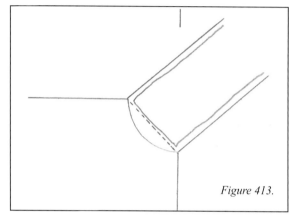

Figure 413.

Next, use a gouge (a chisel with a concave cutting edge) to cut out, in several passages along the stone's entire length, something approaching the concave curve you want. If you have trouble finding a gouge, then you can use a normal chisel whose cutting edge you have ground down to a rounded form.

The curve is finished with a wide chisel. Each of these tools is held as shown in the accompanying drawing, the gouge working along the length of the molding, and the wide chisel perpendicular to it. The curve is verified along its length with a straight edge, and the curve verified with a counter-profile applied at a number of points.

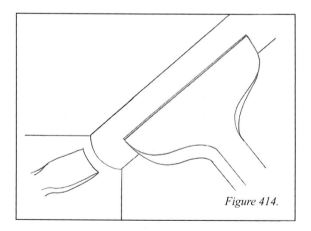

Figure 414.

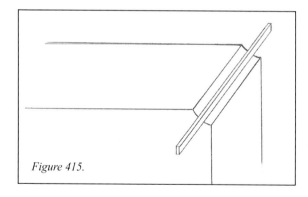

Figure 415.

If you have trouble cutting the curve by eye, you may prefer to first find a line representing its deepest point. This can be done by cutting out a rabbet around a chosen point – or several, if the volume of the concavity is important. But you must be very careful here to not dig too deeply – even by one millimeter – because the line marking the inside of your rabbet would then remain visible on the curve's surface.

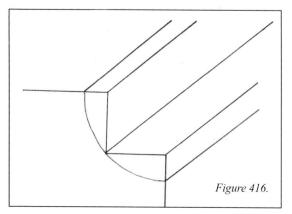

Figure 416.

203

More Complex Moldings

Certain moldings – or combinations – are used frequently in architecture, and have particular names. The *doucine*, shown at right, is an example. It is made up of a carderon and a concavity, one following the other.

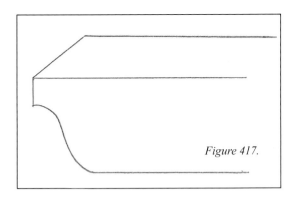

Figure 417.

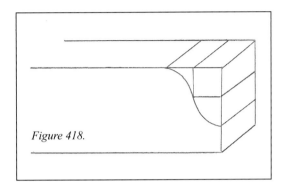

Figure 418.

The block is turned over for marking and cutting. One possible procedure is shown here; it consists of three separate operations: first, a rabbet, next a carderon, and then a concavity.

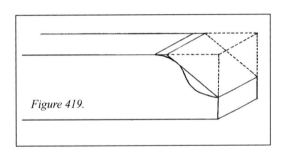

Figure 419.

But another procedure can be used, and will be quicker once you have gotten used to it. This involves drawing an oblique line – a chamfer – starting at the beginning of the molding (top or bottom) and tangent to the curve of the carderon. Once this chamfer is cut, the volumes remaining to be carved out are relatively small.

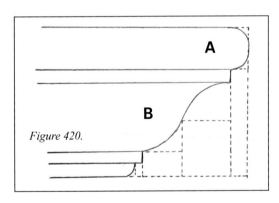

A

B

Figure 420.

Similarly, two possible procedures can be used for this more complex molding. The series of rabbet can be advantageous when there are a number of *filets* (flat bands) in the molding, as at **A** and **B**, because their surfaces are cut and finished when cutting the rabbet concerning them.

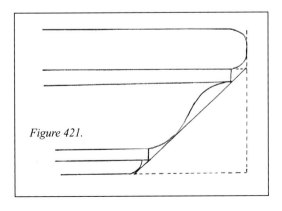

Figure 421.

Otherwise, the stonecutter can draw a chamfer, as for the *doucine* above, which passes through a series of significant points. The advantage of this approach is that the cutting of a chamfer is quicker and easier than cutting a series of rabbets. The disadvantage is that the concavities, carderons, and rabbets still to be done are not symmetrical around an axis, and this must be taken into account when cutting them.

If you are the designer of the molding, you can draw it to have its surfaces and important points aligned; if you are doing a restoration, where you are obliged to follow a model, you will probably find, on studying it, that the stonecutter who designed it several centuries earlier went about it in this way.

Figure 422. Tarragona, Spain

For cutting the molding shown above (figure 422), two possible approaches (at least) exist; one is shown on each side.

ON THE LEFT SIDE: First, a step is cut which will give most of the surface **A**. Another step can then be cut to find some point **B** (chosen arbitrarily) on the concavity. The remainder of the curve will be cut by eye (unless done by an apprentice stonecutter, who may want to find one or two additional points on the curve before trusting his judgment).

ON THE RIGHT SIDE: A chamfer is drawn tangent to the tore and touching the extremities of the concavity (assuming that the design of the molding allows these points to be aligned). The remainder will be done by eye, and checked with a counter-profile.

POINTS D and E, F and G: The deeper these points, the more accentuated is the shadow emphasizing the lines on either side of the tore. It is, though, very difficult to get a chisel very far into such spaces; to deepen the cut, the stonecutter (or his blacksmith) will make a special chisel whose end curves upward from the handle. The cutting must be done by eye, and checked with a counter-profile.

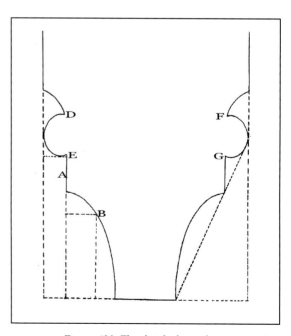

Figure 423. The sketch shows the cross-section of the molding in Figure 368.

205

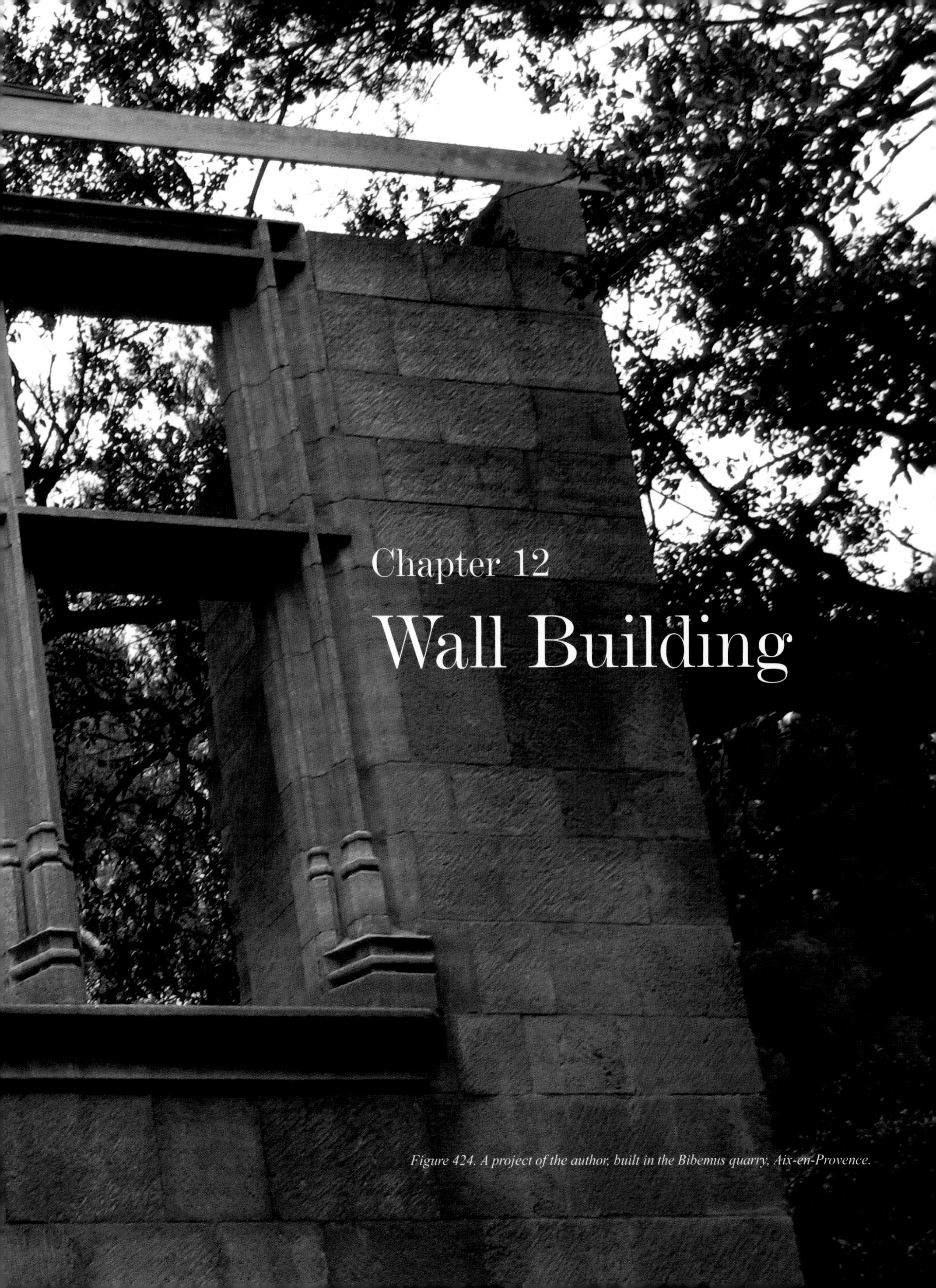

Chapter 12
Wall Building

Figure 424. A project of the author, built in the Bibemus quarry, Aix-en-Provence.

Wall Building

Building with Irregular (Uncut) Stones

The basic principles of wall building are given in Chapter 2, and need not be repeated here. But some additional tips follow:

Alignment of the façade: It is very difficult to build a straight wall by eye alone; even experienced masons use guidelines. These can be set up as follows:
(**NB**: in this example, we take the most usual case: straight walls built at right angles. Any other disposition requires some improvisation with the following method.)
Mark off your building with thin cords stretched taut as shown.

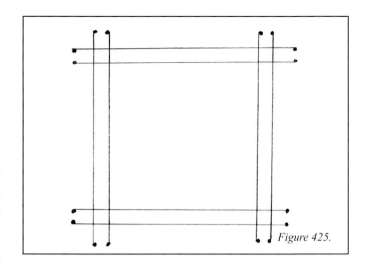

Figure 425.

Each post must be set vertically (with a level or a plumb bob). They should also be consolidated in their vertical position with braces.
The upper line will be moved upward with each course as the wall goes up. The lower one may also be moved, but less frequently.
When viewed from directly above, the two cords will be superimposed. This view, which must be taken as each stone is placed on the wall, gives the vertical alignment (assuming that the posts have been set vertically). The upper cord, which is moved up with each course, gives the alignment along the length of the wall.

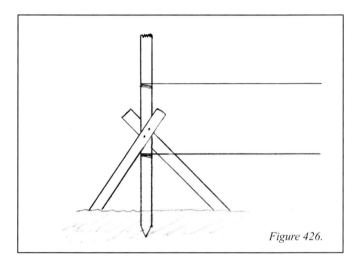

Figure 426.

Should you choose to incline your walls, cut a board (with a straight outside edge) to the inclination chosen. The cut side will be placed against the wall, and the other side should be vertical, as determined with a level or a plumb bob.

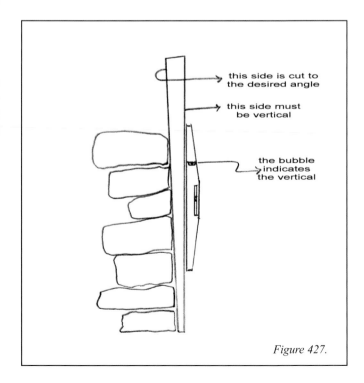

this side is cut to the desired angle

this side must be vertical

the bubble indicates the vertical

Figure 427.

208

As explained in Chapter 2, both inside and outside faces are built, and these are aligned with the cords. The ends of the stones (set to the inside of the wall) can be completely irregular and non-aligned; any spaces will be filled with rubble stones and mortar. Occasional tie or overlapping stones should be used through the thickness of the wall, as at **A and at B** (see also Figure 55 in chapter 2).

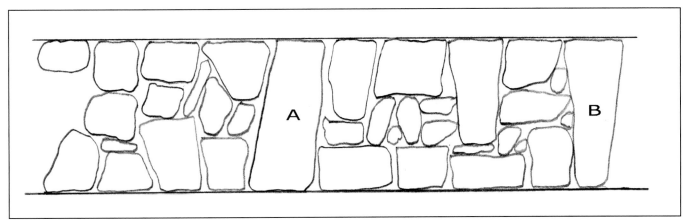

Figure 428. Viewed from above.

On the visible faces, line up any bumps in your stones with the lines – unless you prefer to chip them off – even if most of the surface of the stone will consequently be recessed in relation to the wall's surface. This is the best way to get the irregular faces of hundreds of stones to give the impression of a straight wall.

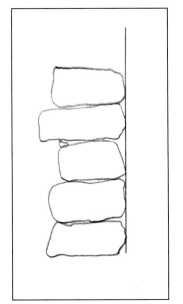

Figure 429. Viewed from the side. (The vertical line is virtual, given by the alignment of the upper and the lower cords as explained on the previous page.)

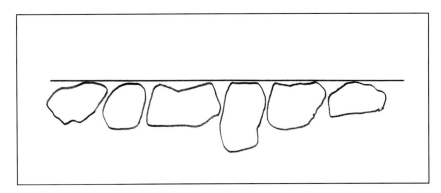

Figure 430. Viewed from above. (The line represents the upper cord.)

If your stones are fairly regular in height, then you can build in courses, using the upper line as a guide for the horizontal alignment of the stones' upper edges. When dealing with cut stone set with very fine joints, this alignment is important (see the following section), but in a rough masonry wall, with joints of about 1/2 inch, you needn't be more than approximate, and if your stones are very irregular, you will not build in well-defined courses at all. Look again at the photos in this book, and at any walls which you admire in your vicinity and which are built with the same kind of stone which is available to you, to help you decide on your masonry style and technique.

Building with Cut Stones (Ashlars)

The masonry techniques used in this case are similar to those used for rough masonry with flat stones, but demand more attention and more precision, in keeping with the precision to which the stones were cut. If the ashlars have been cut to tolerance of only 1.5mm, which is often the case, then the joints will be 3mm, and any deviation will be noticeable. But if the tolerances are more like 5mm, the joints will then be about 10mm, which allows a greater margin for error. Still, we are playing a different and more demanding game here than when using rough stones with irregular edges. It is consequently necessary when setting each stone to verify its alignment in three planes: the vertical, the horizontal, and also in the surface of the wall. (And for the corner stones, each of the two visible surfaces must be aligned in these three planes.)

The Vertical: You can use either a plumb bob or a level with a bubble. The level must lie flat along the stones along its entire length. If this is not the case, you may have to retouch the stone you are about to set (if you see that it is not perfectly square, or that its surface is not perfectly flat), or else retouch the surface of the course to be built on, (if you see that it is not perfectly level).

But if the imperfection is slight, you can probably correct it with the mortar joint. By increasing the thickness of the joint, you can raise the stone; by putting more mortar behind than at the front of the stone (or vice-versa), you can incline it more or less. It is also useful to have lots of small wooden wedges on hand, which you can slip beneath the stone and push in as much as you wish to quickly adjust the inclination. You may also be able to arrange things by dividing the imprecision between two (or more) stones, setting each just slightly out of line and thus avoiding a more noticeable jump in alignment.

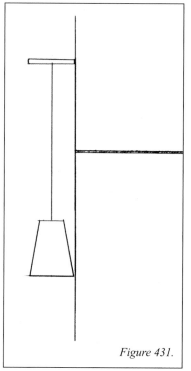

Figure 431.

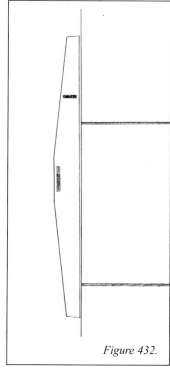

Figure 432.

Aligning the Faces: First, set the corner stones at each of the two ends of the wall as accurately as possible by eye. They should be placed on shims corresponding to the thickness intended for the mortar joint. Then, stretch a thin mason's cord from one to the other. The cord should be two millimeters or more from the stones' surface; you can do this by inserting a matchstick (or anything convenient) between the taut cord and the corner stone. Your alignment is good when the surfaces of the stones are parallel to and equidistant from the cord. Make sure that this is the case for the corner stones before going on to the other stones.

It is best to maintain a slight distance between the cord and the wall because, if the stones were to touch along its whole length, it would be difficult to notice if the cord were pushed slightly out of alignment.

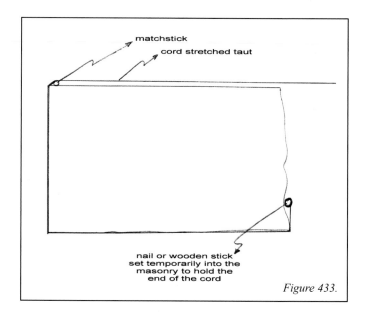

matchstick

cord stretched taut

nail or wooden stick set temporarily into the masonry to hold the end of the cord

Figure 433.

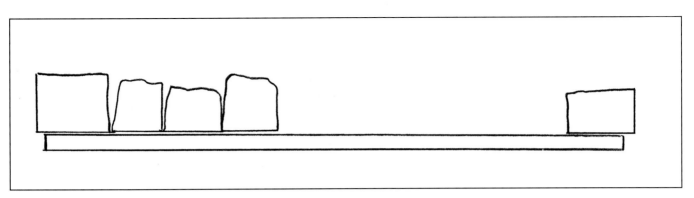

Figure 434. Alignment of the facade with a long rule. Viewed from above.

If you have a straight edge (a board, or an aluminum mason's rule) long enough to go from one end of the wall to the other, you can use this instead of the cord. (But beware of warped boards.) You will then place the edge – held approximately horizontally – against the wall face, just long enough to check the alignment, and then put it aside until the next stone must be checked. This will save you the trouble of setting up the cord at the angles, but it involves a lot of manipulation of the rule – interesting if this is light, but troublesome if it is unwieldy.

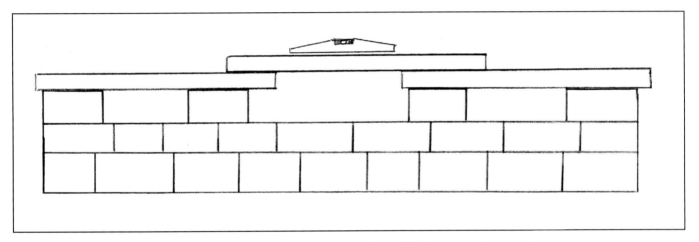

Figure 435. Horizontal alignment of each course, using several rules. Viewed from in front. See also the title page for this chapter.

The Horizontal: This can be checked with the cord used to align the faces, if the cord is placed near the top edge of the course. The upper edges of all the stones can then be aligned, horizontally, with reference to the cord. BUT, due to its weight and flexibility, the cord will nonetheless droop somewhat in the middle, and this must be judged by eye and taken into account.

You may, then, prefer to work partly or entirely with a series of mason's rules. One will suffice when the wall is short enough, but when the wall is longer than the rule, several must be used in the following way:

After setting up and aligning the front surfaces of the corner stones, set up (without mortar) one or more additional stones at intervals along the top of the wall. Set them, like the corner stones, on shims corresponding in thickness to the mortar joint you intend to create. Place rules resting on each pair of these stones. If necessary, adjust the shims so that all the rules are horizontal and in the same plane. You can then fill in the gaps with the other ashlars intended for this course. If need be, the stones holding the rules can be moved somewhat to the right or to the left to create space for the other ashlars as you fill in the gaps.

The last stone in any course will take its place somewhere in the middle, to fill the last short gap left. Perhaps you will find one in your pile of ashlars that measures exactly the length you need, but if not, you must shorten one that has already been cut. Choose the one that needs minimal shortening, and/or is not very thick, or has a receding angle at one end.

211

Setting the stones: Once you have acquired the judgment that comes with experience, you will be able to set your ashlars one by one, directly on the surface of mortar which you deem necessary, and adjust their position quickly before the mortar takes hold. But in the early stages, I find it best to lay out the entire course without mortar, starting from the corners, and verifying the position of each stone as it is put into place and adjusted with shims and/or wedges. When you are satisfied, you can carefully tip the stones back (1/4 rotation, so that they rest temporarily on their rear ends), one by one, and pour the mortar or spread it with a trowel. Then tip each one back again and quickly recheck its alignment. The mortar will not accept more than a few seconds of shifting the stones about, so have some small wooden wedges on hand for rapid adjustments as necessary.

Figure 436.

The Mortar: Make your mortar with enough water so that it is fairly runny. For joints of 3 mm, you must obviously use sand having a lesser granulometry; sift the sand if necessary. For joints even thinner than that, it is better just to pour a thick lime and water mixture without sand onto the surface on which you will set your stones. Moreover, to avoid the dry stones' immediately absorbing the water from the mortar, you should wet down the surface to be sealed before applying the liquid lime.

POSTWORD: Modern Times

The effects of industrialization on stone work

The major effect of industrialization was the large-scale manufacture of substitute materials, such as concrete blocks, or more recently, large hollow bricks. In Europe, these became the usual materials for house building. The wall surfaces, not very esthetically pleasing, are rendered over on the outside (if the builder hasn't run out of money) with a cement-based mortar with a coloring pigment added, and are plastered on the inside. More recently, spray-on or roll-on products are available. In North America, since a century and a half now, houses are usually made using standardized 2 by 4 inch lumber nailed together to form a frame, which can be covered by nailing on one of a variety of industrially manufactured materials; for the interior, the most usual is prefabricated sheets of plaster board, called "dry wall".

For larger buildings meant to impress (banks, police stations, courthouses, houses of government), ashlars were sometimes used throughout the nineteenth and early twentieth centuries both in Europe and America, but most often, big buildings were made of a framework of steel girders assembled with rivets, to which are then attached pre-fabricated panels, usually of either cast concrete, or thick, resistant glass.

For architectures both big and small, such materials are transported from any point on a continent to another with ease, so that architecture is no longer a function of local resources and conditions. This has led to the quasi-disappearance of regional styles. In some places (certain regions or departments in France, for instance), legislation has been put in place to impose certain characteristics of the local traditions on house building, but these usually give only pale copies which don't really resemble their supposed models except in the color schemes imposed. Some architects, working on prestigious projects such as hotels in ski resorts, have been able to find imaginative solutions combining luxury with traditional design and materials, even when the building is many times bigger than those which inspired its design. But because their components are not mass-produced, standardized, and quick to assemble, they cost a lot more to build, and consequently, remain a minority in modern construction.

Nonetheless, stone crafts continue to exist in both Europe and America, albeit with more restricted activity than previous to the mid-nineteenth century when industrial materials became predominant. Some clients prefer stone in spite of the cost; others want at least a narrow facing wall on the outside of a 2 by 4 frame or a block wall. And particularly, in Europe, the restoration and conservation of historical monuments has kept the crafts of stonecutter and sculptor alive.

Evolution in the methods of stonecutting due to the use of machines

In quarries, the extraction is now done with saws mounted on rails. These are normally chain saws with diamond-tipped cutting edges. They cut out blocks of about 2m x 1m x 1m from the mass, and these blocks are further cut up, either at the quarry, or by an artisan stonecutter equipped with personal saws who buys the big blocks at an advantageous price. These saws usually have big discs 50 to 100 cm in diameter) mounted on a rigid frame. Jets of water constantly wash and cool the cutting edges, inundating the cement floor. In some cases the frame moves over a table on which the block of stone lies; in others, the saw is fixed and the table is mobile. In either case, the stone is cut into blocks of the dimensions desired. Only twenty years ago, this could only be done to an accuracy of about 1 cm, but now the imprecision is not more than 2 mm, and the blocks are set square with the same precision.

All this saves a lot of strenuous and not very rewarding (neither creatively nor financially) work in the quarry, and also saves the stonecutter who is making an arch or a molding the time and trouble of squaring the stones at the required dimensions prior to doing the more interesting work. When making ashlars for a wall, nothing more need be done, but it is usual – at least for historical monuments – to redo the visible surfaces with hand tools. This involves, for soft stones, taking off about 2 mm over the entire surface using a stone ax; for hard stones, between 10 and 20 mm, which must be done by pitching and chiselling the edges and then going over the entire surface with a point. This enables the new stones to better match the appearance of the old, which are never smooth but always bear tool or erosion marks.

Most stonecutters have a hand-held disk saw, to which I have an aversion, but I will readily admit that it saves time for those willing to get covered with stone dust. This machine can be used for approaching the finished surface in almost all cases. As it can be used only for straight cuts, the cutter will score the part to be removed, and then knock off the pieces between score marks with a pitching chisel or directly with a hammer. The remaining few mm to the line will be removed with hand tools.

A more recent tool is the pneumatic chisel. This is powered by a compressor and operates a very rapid percussion movement of the chisel end at a speed and through an amplitude which the user can adjust to his needs. The chisel ends can be changed, and are manufactured in all the shapes and sizes of traditional tools. The chisel is held in both hands; one hand near to and directing the cutting edge, the other further back on the controls. This tool enables the user to chisel directly to a line, and no further finishing is required. It vibrates a lot and makes my hands numb.

Some thoughts on traditional hand work and on the use of machines

As you have guessed, I prefer using traditional hand tools. I like the feel of how they react on the stone, I like the movements that my wrist makes to direct the chisel and vary its angle of attack without my even thinking about it, I like chiselling very carefully into delicate spots, and I like knocking off big pieces with powerful blows when rough cutting a surface. I like working outside (most of the time), I don't like cement floors or walls, nor machine noise, nor dust everywhere. I don't want my environment cluttered up with machines and sheds, and for such advantages, I am willing to take a bit more time to earn the money I could earn faster if I created a more work-efficient environment that I disliked.

Certainly, machines help you to make money more quickly, and enable you to have more time for other aspects of life, so I don't wish to tell anyone not to use them. Moreover, it is not necessary to choose between purism and productivism; it is possible to use whatever degree of modern process that seems useful to you, while not using others, according to your feeling. But I think it important that those who want to maintain some distance from an industrialized world realize that it is possible to build or to practise these crafts in a simple fashion, as was done for hundreds of years. This was the craft and the way of life that attracted me when I became aware of its existence over twenty years ago.

I hope then, that this book gives you pleasure to contemplate the beauty of these products of an earlier age, and enables you to better appreciate the skills that went into their realization. Some will, as I did, see themselves as inheritors of this thousand year tradition, and I would be glad to know that it has inspired others and helped their own projects take form.

To further this, I wish to create a website where I can give you any new information I learn, reply to your questions (or leave these open for replies from other readers), and enable you to share your experiences, discoveries, and accomplishments. This website will be common to earth, stone, and wood building.

The address is: www.architrad-books.com

David Campbell,
Aix-en-Provence,
January 8, 2010

Figure 437. The author's workshop.